PORTUGAL

Europe's Best-Kept Secret

By

Sar Perlman

ISBN 9781720126096
Published by Izhar Perlman
zika@sapo.pt
Cadaval - Portugal

PORTO

PORTUGAL

Torres Vedras

Ponte de Sor

Sintra

Cascais

LISBON

Setúbal

Monsaraz

ALENTEJO

Vila Nova
de Milfontes

Odemira

ALGARVE

Monte Gordo

Table of Contents

PROLOGUE

Author's note - January 2014

More than 15 years after this book was published, and despite all of the modernization and Euro-zoneization that Portugal has undergone since then, the country still remains today true to its traditional form - people still stop for a relaxing coffee break mid-day, seafood is still amazing, and while there are bigger and wider highways people still get lost (even with GPS!) In other words... Portugal is still Europe's Best-Kept Secret!

Europe's best-kept secret is such that every year thousands of tourists fail to discover it even after sightseeing its beautiful cities, dining in its traditional restaurants and visiting its historic sites.

I have seen numerous tourists come to Portugal and leave merrily with their collections of pictures and souvenirs, unknowingly missing the entire flavor of the country. After reading this book, you wouldn't be one of those.

If you fear that this is a shallow touristic guide full of trivia or yet another dry and boring information book, put your worries aside. Rest assured that this book is anything but that.

Call it what you will, it is a collection of short stories about people and places, anecdotes illustrating the true life and culture of Portugal and a few minuscule history lessons. In short, it is an action-packed, romantic and humorous portrayal of the forgotten land of discoverers, Portugal.

If you are part of that special breed, the adventurous unguided tourist, who risks his daily life by traveling alone in a foreign country, this book should serve you well.

If "getting into the spirit of Portugal" from your lofty armchair at home is all you desire, this book should suit your needs, being more of an insider's view.

Even if you are one of those unfortunates who due to reasons beyond their control, were forced to listen to monotone, faster-than-light and shallow explanations from a tour guide while travelling in an overbooked bus, there is still hope. This book will arm you with information that most of the others and even some of the guides would not have (no unfair and embarrassing questions which make the guides blush, please,) and possibly provide you and your honey with a chance to make an escapade or two, while the others are still sleeping or watching TV in their room.

The appendix contains a pronunciation guide to

any of the Portuguese words mentioned in the body of the book, with their meanings.

Now, I believe that understanding and respecting the customs, general history and lifestyle of the places I visit makes for a happy hospitality and preserves these values. It is my opinion that ordering a hamburger in a small traditional Portuguese restaurant offends and even corrupts the locals. I have therefore made a point of noting down and explaining most of the local dishes so that you can order with confidence and enjoy these heavenly meals.

From the southern areas of the Alentejo, where time goes slower than the lazy cattle which inhabit its grazing fields, to the northern areas of Porto, where the speeds of automotive vehicles exceeds that of most airplanes, Portugal is uniquely and entirely exotic. A country not Mediterranean nor wholly European, not entirely developed yet ahead of others in many ways, where dictatorship and revolutions were contemporary matters only yesterday, Portugal is indeed full of controversies, tranquilities and impossibilities alike.

Portugal, Europe's best-kept secret, has a lot to offer. If you aren't there already, I hope you will make urgent arrangements to get there when done with this book.

Well, let the adventure begin

Chapter 1
WELCOME TO PORTUGAL...

Hold it!   Even before checking in at your hotel, there are some facts you must know about the people. You will have to converse with people to get directions, request assistance and perhaps ask for your room keys or for extra beach towels.   You may as well get in the groove from the start as to the art of getting what you want in Portugal.

The first thing I learned about Portugal is its special time zone.   It seems as if time has its own rules in this very relaxed country. In its northern regions time might be going two times slower than the western world. As one goes south toward Lisbon, things go twice as slow as up north. From there, the further you head down south, the slower time gets, until at last, *E'pá*! one arrives at the heart of the Alentejo, the southern countryside, where the concept of time barely exists.

I have found that nation-wide, most appointments are set for a tentative date and time. If you are lucky and nothing occurred that day to postpone the meeting to a later date, it would take place approximately half an hour after the actual appointment time.   Why should I mention luck?   As it seems that every remote reason is pounced upon to delay action, and it is by sheer luck that one finds oneself in a meeting as scheduled.

One can easily mistake this to be dislike of foreigners by certain individuals, until one finds that most inhabitants are unpredictable culprits of forgetfulness, even among themselves. The whole country, it seems, behaves this way.

I found that out the hard way. I called up a friend and agreed to meet two days later to have a drink.   That evening had arrived and my friend seemed to have forgotten completely of the entire affair and was otherwise engaged!   I was deeply insulted and gave up on her. A week later she called me up, asking if I was busy the next day. I was not, and so we had a date. We met the next day, as if nothing happened, and we both had a good time. The lesson was that spontaneousness in Portugal is half the battle.

From then on I did just splendidly. I would call up friends only a few hours before the time I wanted to see them and magic!   And I would never take any engagements seriously unless they were confirmed several hours prior to its occurrence, and even then, with some reservation.   I saved myself much heartbreak that way.

Things that take only an hour in the United States might take several hours if not a day in some extreme cases. People move slower, and take their time in doing their tasks. I have discovered that phenomenon to exist in almost any store, bank, gas station and even in some hotels. I say "roll with the punches." Don't take it personally, there is no discrimination. Everyone is treated equally slowly.

For instance, a normal workday would often be: arrive at work around nine in the morning, which really means half past nine ("the traffic was horrible today..."), get things organized for a bit until it is time to go and drink a *café* (a "small coffee" which usually takes anywhere from a quarter to half an hour to drink.) By the time one is back to the office, lunchtime is just around the corner, which could last till three in the afternoon. From there it is a free ride till the next coffee break and then soon after, the end of the day with dinner starting at around eight o'clock. Although the workday is longer, it is far easier and more enjoyable due to the many breaks.

Now I ask you, which is better: running around from nine till five like a chicken with its head cut off, or working leisurely from nine thirty (or thereabouts) to seven with a two hour lunch and a few *cafés* in one's stomach. I am now much more in favor of the latter, even though I have to wait a bit before I get helped. It took me a month before I was relaxed enough to enjoy the excellent and caring service rather than getting irritated and outraged at how slow it was.

A story comes to mind of when I first arrived at the Lisbon International airport which illustrates the above perfectly. The first thing I noticed as soon as I had stepped off the plane was that at once it felt as though I had arrived at another planet. It seemed as if gravity in Portugal was stronger. Lifting one's feet off the ground was not an easy task. Men, women and children, Portuguese and foreign alike, were reluctant to move faster than the earthworm climbs a hill. Even I, Mr. Hurry himself, was strolling, not walking, down the long terminal corridors.

The number of suitcases and bags appearing down the conveyor belt, which descended from its mysterious origin somewhere behind the scenes, could have been counted on one hand for every ten minutes. The carousel carried the few baggage items around even slower. So slow and prolonged was the process, that I found myself dozing off periodically while standing, leaning there against the luggage cart, waiting for my two dear, black and red-trimmed companions to make their grand entrance.

The sound of the carousel stopping woke me up. My suitcases were nowhere in sight. I looked around in vain for any attendants, clerks or any airport employees. A lonely Customs Officer was standing far away on the other side of the spacious baggage claim area. I walked over but hesitated to approach him, his eyes seemed to be closed and I could have sworn I heard a muffled snore. To my surprise, he noticed me immediately and proved to be of assistance.

He explained the way to Lost and Found, hands flying left and right to emphasize each turn. He repeated his directions energetically three times over in varying versions, to make sure I had really got it.   I thanked him profusely and started following his directions. Glancing back over my shoulder I could see the Officer get back to his relaxed position. How strange, I thought, it wasn't even siesta time.

Within minutes I was in the Lost and Found office, if one could call it that. It was a larger room with many bags and suitcases scattered about, and an empty reception counter.   I coughed several times, attempting to attract attention.   Perhaps ten minutes and many coughs later, from behind a colored Plexiglas divider slowly emerged a pleasant looking woman who, upon arriving at the counter, asked how she could help me. I contained myself and instead of reprimanding her sluggish behavior, told her about my long wait at the baggage claim area and the absence of my luggage. She asked for my name and if I had a luggage stub.

"Perlman, Sar Perlman," I answered and handed over my plane ticket, to which the luggage voucher was attached.

"Pedro?"   she asked. I got really confused. How did Perlman turn into Pedro was beyond me. She looked at my ticket.

"Oh! Perlman!" she cried, as if she was expecting me, and began to search through the heaps of suitcases and packages. Within minutes I was happily reunited with my baggage.   She apologized for the inconvenience and warmly welcomed me to Portugal, her large and friendly smile melting away any irritation I had felt.

Both she and the Customs Officer took their time, but they had helped me in a cordial and easy-going fashion, and without rancor or complaints. How could one become angry with such amiable people?   You can't. I thanked her and left with my loaded cart.

I remember sitting in a small café in Lisbon, drinking a *carioca de limão*. An old balding man who was sitting at a table close by drained the morning caffeine dosage from a tiny white cup. He was conversing with the owner/waiter (most of them are the same in the really small cafés) who was behind the counter, repeatedly and aimlessly passing a soft rag over the metal top of the pastries display.   It was a rather loud conversation and so everyone in the room was included.

"I am supposed to be attending an important meeting at the moment," remarked the balding elder with a grunt, "rather than sitting here, drinking a coffee."

"Why don't you hurry on over to your appointment then?" asked the owner with curiosity.

The oldster shrugged and responded with a shrewd Portuguese saying: "If my mother waited nine months for me to come out, that guy can wait too!" We all had a good laugh.

The second secret to Portuguese interpersonal relationships is that in Portugal there is no such thing as a big city. Even the biggest city, is in fact a small village in disguise.

Everyone knows everybody and each person you will meet is most likely to quickly bring you into the friends category. The Portuguese are a very, and I mean extremely, friendly and lively bunch. To assume the same attitude brings a higher percentage of success in all of your dealings.

However, to criticize Portugal or to pass judgement on Portuguese customs can bring about the most astonishing reaction. I shall advise to keep any negative opinions to yourself if you value your Portuguese acquaintances' friendship.

The Portuguese I have met were very touchy about their country and tradition. They might tell you all about their own shortcomings. They might even joke at times about their imperfections, but as soon as you, a foreigner, join in with any negative opinions, the game's over and the friendly attitude shuts down at once. Strangely, the Portuguese tend to complain the hardest about those things they most love and appreciate.

I distinctly recall my first night out in Cascais. I went out for a drink and, over a beer and a small bowl of peanuts, started a conversation with a friendly Portuguese who was sitting next to me at the bar and spoke a bit of English. Before I knew it I was encouraged to phone him soon to make arrangements to meet again for another drink. Two days later I did call him and we agreed to meet in the same bar later that evening. However, at that time, I was unaware of the eccentricities of the tempo in Portugal, and innocently showed up on time. I left twenty minutes later, frustrated. Had I waited another ten minutes, certainly he would have turned up.

I was down in the southern beach of Monte Gordo in the Algarve one sunny afternoon. It was a beautiful beach, the golden strip a few kilometers long, lounge chairs and sun umbrellas planted in several long and quasi-orderly lines, vendors of pastries and ice creams roaming about, calling out the nature of their merchandise.

I was enjoying the extremely cold water around my lower half and the hot sun baking my upper half. Another young ocean-lover was floating a few yards away, enjoying life just like I was. I started by asking a few questions, and after some minutes we were deep into conversation about the wide differences between the north and the south of Portugal (he was from the north...) the cool waves disrupting our chat occasionally. Soon we parted, blue-lipped and shivering, having agreed to meet five minutes later at the café right by the beach entrance.

This time, knowing how slow the Portuguese Father Time walks, I unhurriedly dried myself, waited approximately a quarter of an hour and began heading towards the meeting zone, again unhurriedly. We arrived there together, both late but happy, and lingered over coffee, the entire view of the beach in front of us. We even made arrangements to go out that evening to capture Monte Gordo by night. Needless to say, I observed the timing rules to the letter and added some spontaneous changes to the plan. We partied till dawn, and had Monte Gordo's nightlife extended past six o'clock in the morning, I am sure we would have partied on.

The last yet very important fact to keep in mind, is that the first reply to any request which is the least bit unusual, is "*Não*" which means "no". This, however, is not always final, no matter how official it sounds. If one persists and discusses one's problems and difficulties long enough and preferably with many different clerks, the solution might present itself magically. "All of a sudden" your request will get processed. Although frequently successful, this maneuver is not guaranteed.

Some workers, especially the customer service representatives, hate to stick out their neck for unusual requests. They feel much safer responding with a *Não*. This, you might say, directly contradicts what I mentioned earlier about friendliness, but not so. You see, as long as your request is routine and covered by the boss' instructions the service you receive will often be excellent. But, once confronted with a decision to make, your customer service officer could turn into a tortoise and fold his head and limbs inside his house faster than you can say Jacksonville. It is knowing that this phenomenon exists, and faced with it, ignoring the authoritative *Não* and repeating your request in another manner or tone or to another person, which might win the day.

This applies only to the shady areas, never to the requests which are strictly prohibited by rules. Remember, the tortoise will fold his flippers at any hint of uncommon requests, but the scent of direct violations of regulations will send your tortoise away in a flurry, never to return again.

Example: It was the end of March and I wished to extend my stay by a week.   I went to the airline counter in the Lisbon airport.   The lady behind the glass divider studied my ticket for an extended period of time. First came a decisive *Não*, and then an official mutter that in order to change the flight date, I would have to pay the difference between my fare and the current normal fare, a substantial amount of six hundred dollars. She was about to dismiss me and attend to the next customer, hoping his case would be routine and normal. I didn't give up easily. I informed her that in Miami, my travel agent assured me that I could delay my flight for a minimal fee, and you can hardly call six hundred dollars minimal. Alas, my plea fell on deaf ears.

So off I went, steaming and frustrated, to a local travel agent, and presented her with my problem. She took up the project and a couple of hours later, after many phone calls and discussions with airline officials, she had my flight changed to the later date and said the fee would be a hundred and fifty dollars, which I should pay at the airport counter the day before I leave. Big difference. I thanked her immensely and she went back to her phone, cheerful and contented. And she didn't even charge me for the service.

The related manifestation, which cannot go unmentioned, is named the *colega*. It means a colleague or fellow worker. I first heard of it when calling a company's representative to inquire about some of their offered services. The number I was given for her was constantly busy and so I called the main number.

The receptionist answered with a high pitched voice, and I told her I wanted to speak to Silvia. She asked who was calling.

"Perlman, Sar Perlman," I replied.   She put me on hold and came back a second later.

"Mr. Pedro, Ms. Silvia is on the Internet. Could you try her number again in five or ten minutes please?" There was that "Mr. Pedro" again. This time I had no means of showing her how it was spelled, so I dropped it. I just resignedly asked if a message could be sent to Her Highness Silvia, for her to call me back.

Of course, the tiny voice answered, but since Silvia's office was on the fifth floor and the reception desk was located on the ground floor, she would have a *colega* take up the message. I thanked her approvingly and disconnected.

Later on, when I called again, the receptionist, surprised, asked if I hadn't received a call back yet. No, I hadn't. Oh, my *colega* must have misplaced the message, she said. This time she will send it up with a more trusted *colega*. I sighed and hung up.

The skinny on this one is that *colega* does not necessarily exist. It could be a fictitious name created to establish an anonymous identity which would serve as a scapegoat. If the message did not get relayed, "oh, my *colega*..." If a duplicate key did not fit the lock it was supposed to open, "oh, my *colega*..." If a project was too burdensome, "I will relay this to my *colega*..." So, beware of this mysterious, unproductive and sometimes non-existent fellow.

A good way to handle this is to politely ask for the *colega*'s name, and suddenly, tasks get done faster and better (I think my popularity in Portugal just sank to the bottom of the Atlantic, as this secret tool might rob many people of their proud excuse for not having done their job on time. But, I am willing to sacrifice for the sake of my readers.... Also, now that I think of it, I have just decided against translating this book into Portuguese.)

Well, this just about does it. Now that you are armed with these invaluable and powerful techniques, you can go ahead and check into your hotel and get settled in.

The Portuguese traffic easily rivals, in regards to the amount of stunts and suspense, any of those Hollywood-produced action-movies. It is not my intention to discourage you from driving there. On the contrary, if you can somehow arrange for a car while you are there, get one by all means. All I am trying to do is minimize the initial shock.

The first rule, which I think holds firm at all times and under any circumstances on any Portuguese road, whether wide or narrow, a freeway or a one-way street, is "always expect one thing: the unpredictable."

Near-Death-Experience is the only expression which springs to mind to adequately describe my personal first encounter with the Portuguese traffic. I was lured into the trap by my father when he picked me up from the airport (he lives in Portugal,) and I will never forgive him for not warning me earnestly of what was to come. He did say, off-handedly, that driving in Portugal was not quite like anywhere else except, perhaps, Italy. But somehow it did not register properly. Nor did it even vaguely prepare me for the tiger which hid in what was supposedly a little cub's lair.

You see, I was just getting adjusted to the slow pace prevailing all around, but for whatever reason, on the road, the pace swings from one extreme to the other. Vehicles have only one speed: the maximum. As soon as we took off, I realized I was actually in the back of a racing car, in the midst of a Formula One event.

I must have held my breath the entire trip. Tiny Fiats, Opels and other similar European compact cars, were passing us left and right at an unimaginable speed, repeatedly missing us by inches. I was clawing the seat with my nails as a fleet of miniature motorscooters of Italian origin, named Vespa, whizzed by our right and cut immediately in front of us. Coming into a traffic circle, one of many in Portugal, I gasped as our red Alfa Romeo lurched ahead while a BMW coming around the roundabout lane, was heading straight on course for collision with our stern, missing us by less than an inch. My heart was beating either so rapidly or so slowly, I couldn't even register a pulse.

Then we came onto the *auto-estrada*, the freeway. The maximum speed which I earlier described proved to be a mild stepping-stone to what lay ahead. I vividly recall that sign which clearly said 120 in black and red, supposedly signifying the speed limit. Others must have confused it to be the minimum speed, as not one car on the road was going slower than 130 kilometers an hour. A Mercedes passed by at an incredible speed of what seemed like 160, the air turbulence it created shaking our car. It was being chased by a small Peugeot, which was constantly flashing its lights at the Mercedes, signaling it wished to overtake. The Mercedes, insulted, suddenly sped off into even higher speeds, attempting to shake the little rascal off its tail.

But the Peugeot was following closely behind. Way ahead, an old Renault 5 was peacefully moving right into their lane, unaware of what was approaching rapidly from behind. A second later, a stealthy sports motorcycle passed by, scaring the heck out of me. It was going faster than the Mercedes and the Peugeot.   I closed my eyes, not desiring to be the witness of the unavoidable horrible accident. But, nothing occurred. Amazingly they all came out fine.

You may consider 130 kilometers small change, when in Germany they drive as fast as their Porsches can go. I have been to Germany, and it is the land of law and order whereas Portugal is the opposite. And 300 kilometers an hour in Germany is equal to 130 in Portugal. Test it for yourself if your heart is up to it.

After a quarter of an hour of driving down the *auto-estrada*, we got off to a road which connects Lisbon and Cascais, at which point my heart took the opportunity to dislodge itself and found its way down under the seat where it was safe. The road was following the coastline, where we were practically driving on the beach. Its name is usually mentioned with a whisper, "the *Marginal*."

Up to a few years ago, when finally several traffic lights were installed along its four curved and narrow lanes, drivers would go as fast as they could, daring Death to catch them if it could. The four lanes sometimes transform into two and as if that was not bad enough, the two-way traffic is only divided by a thin white stripe. This road is much safer now, I was glad to hear.

This route does, however, carry a collection of impressive seascape views along its way, possibly a contributing factor to the accident rate. I strongly advise when motoring down its crooked path, to pull off the road and safely appreciate the magnificent scenery.

This road is also a surfing attraction. In rough weather conditions, especially in winter, some sections of it are sometimes subject to waves -- yes, sea waves -- climbing over the rocks and breaking over the roofs of the travelling cars. Though I had driven by these parts back and forth in hope of going through this incredible and dangerous experiment myself, I have never managed to personally experience it, and so am forced to relay it in its simplicity to the readers.

My reliable sources described to me the procedure for surfing the *Marginal*, but I advise the readers this is a matter for professionals only and should not be attempted at home. If you do get caught in it, however, it is jolly good to know what to do. You will see the waves coming over the road ahead of you. You will remember reading about it in this book and commence emergency surfing procedure:

1) Roll up the windows...

2) Switch on the windshield wipers at full speed.

3) Don't brake hard -- the road will be slippery and the visibility poor, so the driver behind you might not see that are braking. Best is to slow down gradually to a moderate speed.

4) Hold on while the wave breaks on your rooftop.

5) Advance slowly during the intervals between the waves until you are safely out of range.

There you have it, surfing the *Marginal*. And if you see someone desperately driving back and forth over these sections of the road, trying to catch a wave, you will know it is I...

Back to my journey. I survived the highways, the roundabouts and the *Marginal*. Just when I thought it was safe, a looming menace called the narrow one-way street crept up on me from the dark. These ancient and stealthy creatures are still alive and kicking in most cities, towns and villages across Portugal.

They seem harmless at first, smoothly pulling you in, attracting your attention with the old yet aesthetic houses decorating both of its sides, and then they strike.

As one drives down the narrow alley, the houses at the end of the street suddenly seem to expand and close in. You get nervous, concerned about the width of the car, not quite sure if it would fit. You slow down and watch the edges of the houses reaching out towards your vehicle. You conclude it won't fit and look back in the rearview, determined to reverse. Only now there is another car behind you, patiently waiting for your forward progress. You decide to go forward and save yourself the embarrassment of having to explain to the driver behind how you went down a road too narrow for your car's size. So into first gear again, and if you are in luck you go through unscratched.

The solution is to rent a compact car or, if you are a proud owner of a BMW 850i, not to drive down narrow one-way streets.

And here is the real clincher. A story was told to me by a friend, whose identity I will not reveal (I try to be kind to my sources.)   Her neighborhood consisted of many blocks of old, narrow alleys which formed a complex maze only locals could navigate. One bright day, the local police decided to put order into this labyrinth (I guess too many policemen got lost there.)   They turned every alley into a one-way street and put up conspicuous signs at the appropriate places. My friend and her neighbors returned home that day to find they had to make a detour around seven blocks of one-way streets just to get home.   Guess what happened?   The next morning, a strategically placed one-way street sign was missing. The perplexed police force immediately rectified the situation by putting another sign up, only to find it gone as well the next morning. The war went on for several weeks with the toll of cut up one-way road signs steadily increasing, until finally the police gave in. "Not every narrow one-way street is indeed a one-way street," is the moral of that story.

Well, we eventually reached our destination, Cascais, and I got out of the car, trembling but proud. After that ride, the wildest rollercoaster in existence would seem boring. We parked along one of the close-by streets, about twenty yards away from home. Our two-story apartment building, painted bright yellow with deep green decorating the window and door frames, was overlooking an intersection of five small roads. I looked around in confusion, trying to determine whether that was really an intersection or a parking lot. Cars were parked in every possible location, and in every conceivable way. On the sidewalk, halfway up the pavement, on the sides of the road and even in the middle of the intersection!

Skyrocketing car sales, narrow streets and lack of parking spots, forced all to cope with the parking problem. One comfort is that the police does not make a big issue out of it, e.g. the police usually gives orders to tow away only those cars parked in a marked no-parking zone or those that literally block the road. After all, why punish the people if there simply isn't enough parking space? Of course, if the neighbors call up and complain about it, the police is forced to order an illegally parked car to be towed, but that does not occur too often.

I was informed that on summer weekend nights, one could not find a parking space closer than several hundred feet away from home. I gasped as having my own private garage in Florida I was never concerned with finding a parking spot.

Though rarely displaying it, the Portuguese

frequently complain of a "disease" called stress. Even so, they would never admit that the way they drive and the complications involved in finding a parking spot have anything to do with it.

I lay in bed that night pondering this puzzle. Finally, just prior to escaping to the land of dreams, it occurred to me that life without some action and risk (and the ability to complain about it) is not really life. And in Portugal, traffic has definitely earned its name as a supplier of those last two necessities.

Chapter 2
FROM THE MOUTH OF HELL
TO THE MOUNTAIN OF THE MOON

Unbeknownst to the majority of Mankind, there is a definite path from the Mouth of Hell to the Mountain of the Moon. It is an exact one, never to be deviated from under any circumstances. It is quite useful to know this route (and not because any of us will end up in hell, I hope) as well as fantastically enjoyable to travel it.

Before embarking upon this odd but pleasant journey, it is important to first reach the starting line, which happens to be that most fearful place: the Mouth of Hell (bloodcurdling background music starts now.)

Travelling west from Cascais on the *estrada da Boca do Inferno*, passing over an ancient bridge, where a tiny sea inlet washes against a castle's stone foundations, soon old and magnificent mansions appear on the right while the sea washes against the rocks to one's left.

A cluster of restaurants and coffee shops signals the landing zone. It's at this innocent location, the signs announce everywhere, that the *Boca do Inferno*, the Mouth of Hell, is situated. Only in Portugal is coffee served even at Hades' doorstep, I chuckled at the thought as I stood there, facing the numerous signs offering coffees and pastries.

A distant rumble followed by a hiss turned my joyful mood into a more cautious one. What was that?

"What you hear is nothing compared to the fiercest winter days," commented a local shop owner with a smile. "You should come here in December, when the sparks really fly."

Coming around the restaurant's white walls and climbing the stairs, a large area full of jagged rocks revealed itself. Sculptured by wind and rain, they were gray skeletons of what once used to be solid and round stones.

Suddenly, a wave of spray and foam shot up out of nowhere as if the rocky tract had a large, hidden mouth. A second later, the jagged set of jaws closed up, leaving a cloud of mist hanging in the air.

I moved closer slowly and carefully. A moment later, again without warning, the mouth opened up again and droplets filled the sky above me. A few more forward steps and I stood at the edge of a wide hollow. Below me, the steep walls of the hole dropped abruptly sixty feet down to the rough talus at the bottom. Much like a bridge, the wall nearest the ocean had a large opening at its feet, allowing the sea into the miniature cove.

It appeared the ocean had dug under the rock for

decades and eventually a section of the top layer collapsed, leaving this intriguing creation of Nature in place. At the bottom of the large crevice, rocks varying in shape, size and even color served as the launching pad for the charging waves. The waves would break loudly against them and explode in all directions with force and splendor.

Uninhibited by the sporadic shoals, the waves entering the inlet were not beach waves but Atlantic Ocean swells, tall and powerful. The spray would shoot up more than seventy feet, I calculated with fascination.

The name suited the location very well, I concluded. I didn't care to imagine the experience of getting caught between the waves and the rocks down below. And if Hell resembled what was below me, it certainly made one think twice before sinning.

Walking about half a kilometer west along the coast, an area of gravel and stone stretched out above a cliff. A hot dog stand, plastic chairs and tables were set about, offering a magnificent view. An ancient stairway, I was told, was well hidden nearby. I found it, the low silver rail giving it away. It descended down some steps and disappeared around the cliff.

I climbed down with curiosity. Once round the jagged wall, the stairs went a dizzying seventy feet down to a sloping rocky plateau which formed a beach of sorts. The high-tide line was marked with seaweed, dark barnacles and white salt stains. A few fishermen were sitting here and there, snoozing while watching over their fishing rods.

The smell of the sea was strong and fresh, the sun was warm and the breeze was soft and cool. What a perfect, hidden and romantic spot, I thought. I decided to return there one evening. The sea by night at this quasi-beach must be dazzling. Or, depending on the tide, very wet.

I walked back along the water, and showing respect to Mother Nature's artistic abilities, paid the Mouth of Hell a final visit. I hopped in my car to begin my journey to the Mountain of the Moon.

Driving along the *estrada do Guincho*, the view changed considerably into a breathtaking panorama. The coast was made of jagged and irregular rocky cliffs and crags, the sand and small bushes covering their tops. The ocean, on the left, was embracing the coast with its dark blue arms, miniature white caps forming here and there. The waves, three to four feet tall were breaking repeatedly against the rocks, majestically sending white foam up into the air.

To the right, small trees and bushes were decorating the wild fields of grass and weeds. The green hues varied tremendously from treetop to treetop. The brownish tints of land and sand mixed together on both sides of the narrow and bumpy road made me feel as if I had gone back a few centuries in time, when the traces of human touch were not visible at every corner.

A left turn into a dirt passageway lead me to my next stop, *Furnas do Guincho*. The restaurant sat atop a lower crag, hidden from view, practically hanging over the water. I chose a table out on the balcony, from where

I could view across the River Tejo bay. The opposite bank formed similar scenery of precipices surrounded by clouds of mist and spray. Five or six tiny fishing boats floated about in different strategic spots, their nets collecting fish under the water detectable only by the white and yellow buoys wiggling around each boat.

I sat back and relaxed, the rhythmic sound of the waves soothing me into a serene state of mind. The waiter showed up a few minutes later, carrying a basket of fresh bread, a small plate of green olives and another plate of butter and cheese.

I tasted a bit of each. The thick, delicious bread was still warm, the fresh cheese melted in my mouth, and the olives had a strong and rich taste. It was a surprisingly savory mix. The red wine arrived soon afterwards, and the soothing liquid slowly worked its way into my system. At first, I thought it was a light wine, but a minute or so later, I had already begun feeling light-headed.

Whereas I had been in Hell only half an hour earlier, it now seemed, with the excellent wine, the delicious food and the sea stretching afar to kiss the clear-blue sky at the horizon, that I had suddenly arrived in Heaven. I sat there for quite some time, listening to nature's melody and song, the adrenaline draining out slowly but surely, till at last I was completely at peace with the world.

Alas, one couldn't remain in heaven for long, having eaten the fruit. Even if one paid for it.

I was soon on my way.

The road continued westwards for some time and then turned north. The rocky cliffs were suddenly replaced by a sandy beach, revealing the Guincho in all its splendor. Internationally renowned for its excellent surfing conditions and its strong winds, this short stretch of sand, not even one kilometer long, was packed with surfers, windsurfers and sunbathers. Cars were parked all along the wooden fence that marked the beginning of the beach, and all along the other side of the road, turning the already narrow road into a cramped traffic jam. But it was a lively and energetic event, with smiling faces and merry greetings at every turn.

I decided to make an unscheduled stop. One couldn't travel to the Mountain of the Moon without a snack. On the beach side of the fence, several older women were standing behind their stands, colorful parasols protecting them and their merchandise from the baking sun. White paper packages lay in a pyramidal heap atop the counters. Inside the wrapping were five delicious *Queijadas de Sintra*, a sweet pastry made of cheese, flour and sugar (Sintra is the city of their origin, and where one finds, naturally, the best q*ueijadas*.) These delightful bite-sized cakes, coupled with a cold *sumol de ananás* -- Portugal's popular soft drink -- made a refreshing snack on a hot day, and since it was, I consumed my snack complete.

Heading further north, the road led up to the mountains of *Serra de Sintra*. I was astonished at how diverse the scenery was, all within a radius of not more than twenty kilometers, and only fifteen minutes away from Cascais.

Travelling through the range of Sintra mountains (if one could actually call them mountains, they should be more appropriately termed tall hills,) I watched with amazement as thick forest trees began appearing and soon filled both sides of the road. Large pine trees, wild bushes and dense brush covered the entire ground throughout the forest. I could not however ignore the beauty of Mother Nature's creation, as unsystematic and disorderly as it was. Not only had wilderness prevailed, but vigorously so. One could sense the intensity with which the trees and plants were growing.

A mile of winding and curvy roadways later, the forest was still embracing me. Suddenly, I arrived at a roundabout. A café and a few buildings revealed themselves on the opposite side. Although abrupt, the transition from a forest to a village was a peaceful one. Unlike many places I have been to, Man was not heartlessly encroaching upon Nature's territory. Instead, Man and Nature lived together in harmony, each compromising a bit to aid the other. The buildings were erected all right, but the wild bushes and outgrown weeds were in full bloom, undisturbed, wherever there was room.

Turning left and following the serpentine road, I was travelling down the *estrada do Cabo do Roca*. One couldn't go too long without a drink, I reasoned. And since I hadn't had a *carioca de limão* yet that day, a catastrophe in the making, I pulled in to a small café named "*Bar Moinho Don Quixote*" (the Don Quixote's Windmill Bar.) I passed through the ancient gate and arrived in the small gravel parking lot.

An old windmill was located at the edge of the lot, its round structure restored and kept up in excellent condition. It was obvious it wasn't operational, its "wings" stripped down and secured with a heavy rope to prevent any movement. Though completely useless, the windmill was not destroyed but on the contrary, it was preserved. The Portuguese have a strong sense of tradition. It stirred a sentimental nostalgia in me.

Sitting at the large outside patio, sipping a *carioca de limão* and nibbling on a toast, I was listening to the intense silence. Birds chirped occasionally and the waiter visited me infrequently, thus the quietude was rarely disturbed. The River Tejo's estuary stretched in the distance, its traffic, noise and signs of civilization far away. My gaze was dragged involuntarily across the ocean over to the distant horizon, the vast blue expanse filling a hitherto unknown void in my soul.

Dangerous, I thought to myself. Those hidden corners of natural beauty could easily hypnotize one. I finally managed to pry myself out of my seat and get back to my journey.

Getting back to the main road I took the next right turn and started the ascent toward Peninha. The half-road, half-trail went up at a twenty-five degree angle for quite some time, the countless craters and abysses in the way not making it any easier. I'd give half of my fortune (it's not that much, by the way) for a four-wheel drive vehicle, I told myself, climbing up the obstacle course in my tiny Fiat.

However, when I saw a small Opel coming down the bumpy hill at full speed, its driver and his girlfriend happy as cats in a milk bottling factory, I figured nothing could stop a Portuguese when it came to enjoying the outdoors. "Take advantage of what one has and enjoy every second of it" seemed to be the prevalent frame of mind. I decided to adopt it and enjoy the view instead of complaining.

I stared out the window at the thick vegetation, astounded at how the ground was utterly covered with various ferns, berry plants and plain weeds. Every inch was being occupied. Even the tree trunks were concealed with climbing plants and lichen.

When all of a sudden I could make out the outline of something large and bulky in the distance. Could it really be? I braked hard, my Fiat screeching to a standstill. I stepped out and approached the strange object. Yes, it was a huge boulder, covered with moss and ivy. Perhaps ten feet high and twenty feet wide, this round, gigantic pebble-stone was sitting innocently in between the trees, pretending to be part of the forest. How did that rock get there, why was it so perfectly curved and how long had it been there, were the immediate questions that came to mind. As I continued the climb, pondering this puzzle, more of those oddly shaped boulders presented themselves along the way.

Later on, I learned these were granite rocks of sixteen or so million years ago which got eroded through the millennia by wind, rain and humidity, and since granite erodes in an unusual way -- it becomes round -- those rocks became the egg-like boulders of today.

I finally surmounted the small Everest and made it to the top. A *pousada* was situated on the very edge of the bald hilltop, almost extending over thin air. The rest of the clearing offered several spots from which the general public could admire the spectacular view.

To my right, the sea stretched far into the distant horizon while to my left I could see as far as Lisbon. The sight was indeed impressive. The red roof tops of Lisbon's suburbs were squeezed tightly in the distance, their various shapes and sizes forming a sort of an enormous, colorful quilt.

The nearby mountaintops were covered with low-hanging clouds, creating an atmosphere of mystery and suspense. The absolute silence, only seldom broken by a distant bark of a dog far away, molded that esoteric view into a peaceful and relaxing environment. Breathing in the fresh, cool air, the distinct scents of nature filling my nostrils, I could feel the wilderness around me.

As I descended and continued my travels through the dirt roads, I noticed there was something special about that forest. It seemed good-natured and safe, as if little fairies were watching over me (don't worry, I haven't lost my senses -- it was just a general feeling.)

About twenty minutes later I arrived at the town

of Sintra, where I immediately stopped at *Café Natália*, an excellent local café, to take a *carioca de limão* break. It seemed like ages had passed since I had one. Accompanying the nearly boiling drink came a *travesseiro de Sintra*, another delicious local pastry. Best consumed in Sintra, this light confection was made of sweet and thin, flaky dough filled with squash. And lots of sugar, I forgot. But still, I recommend it wholeheartedly.

Evening was setting in and the sunlight was gradually fading away, painting the street with the magnificent hue of twilight. It was time to embark upon the final and most impressive stretch of my trip.

Sintra, the Mount of the Moon, was given its name by the Romans, which evolved from "Cynthia," the Latin name of the moon goddess. Archaeological excavations produced evidence of what is believed to be lunar worship since the early Copper Age. Moon-shaped chest ornaments were found in some burial caves of those times.

Later on, Roman sun and moon worship courts were discovered around the area, and then Visigothic remains from the sixth century strongly suggest they too worshipped the moon there. Currently there are rumors of secret moon-worship cults in existence around Sintra. Why was this beautiful city such a magnet for moon worshippers dating back to the late pre-historic era?

Additionally, some believed that somewhere in the range of Sintra Mountains, the tunnel that leads to the center of the earth existed. Witches and druids travel to Sintra from around the world. Not too long ago, a shower of stones and pebbles came down on one specific house in Sintra. The police came while it was still "pouring" but no source was ever found for this mysterious rain. Why was this charming town a center for mysticism and the supernatural?

To understand why, I was told by many, one must go and visit Sintra at night. By day it seemed like an innocent normal city, however with the evening came a different view.

The ever-curving and hilly streets of the ancient city, snaked ahead in different directions, chasing each other up and around the foothills. The humidity and mist dimmed the already faint illumination a few existing lampposts shed upon the roads, giving the appearance of times when streets were lighted by flambeaus alone.

The ancient houses whispered forgotten stories of their noble and knightly inhabitants centuries ago while the dark-gray cobbled roads told of long-ago tales about the kings and crusaders which traveled upon them.

Moorish structures blended in with churches, palaces sat amongst simple and cramped dwellings, the present mixed in with the past, while the diffused twilight enveloped the whole lot with a mysterious and enchanting atmosphere. People could be seen here and there, walking about, drinking coffees in cafés, entering and leaving various shops. But that was no modern city. Calm, quiet and relaxed, I would have mistaken it for a medieval town if it wasn't for the stylish French and Italian fashion everywhere. The city itself seemed to come alive and speak of its rich and cultural past.

Where the town edges kissed the beginnings of the forest, haze and vapor engulfed me at once. *Serra de Sintra*, with its microclimate of a green house, was a heaven for anything botanical. The incredibly thick and varied vegetation grew and flourished in a magnificent way.

At the top of the mountain, overlooking the surrounding valley and built more than a thousand years ago, the Moorish castle was covered by fog, its silhouette barely discernible. Following the dateless path of the Portuguese king who once used to live in that fortified palace, the road was a long and winding one. Over hundreds of years, ivy and moss had covered almost entirely the man-made stony walls on both sides of the road, making the rocks seem like part of the vegetation.

Those high fences separated and divided the mountainsides into *quintas* (large mansions with lands) which belonged to the nobles of the king's court. These properties were huge in size, stretching across acres upon acres.

The trees, towering over the road, blocked whatever afterglow remained of the evening, and the route, lacking street lamps, was dark and eerie. The complete silence was broken only by the sound of distant bird chirping and the condensation drops rolling off the tree leaves, creating acoustic effects of a drizzle. It was as if I was indeed in the fifteenth century.

Standing in front of a large metal gate, I surveyed

the entrance to *Quinta de Santo António da Serra*. A stately three-story mansion stood tall and wide, its walls and numerous support pillars covered with climbing plants. The structure had been renovated recently but had retained its four centuries old look. And it was kept in a relatively good condition.

And then, the spookiest feeling crept up on me. Standing there by the side of the road, looking ahead, I could have sworn I saw the apparition of a knight in full armor on his dark horse, galloping toward me, a sizeable sword in his hand, ready to be used in need. My heart skipped a beat and I nearly darted off in search of cover. But then the image dissipated into thin air. I sighed with relief. Though extremely real, it was an optical illusion after all, merely a play of shadows.

Perhaps the lunar influences might not be a legend after all. I quickly got in my car and drove off, heading back home. All the while I was driving, I could feel the magic in the air. And then, once I actually left Sintra and its surrounding *quintas*, the aura of intrigue and glamour vanished unexpectedly and the roads, trees, and houses returned to their normal and boring facades.

Visiting Sintra at night was truly a spiritual experience, reminding me that indeed there were higher things than simple existence in our material universe. And maybe you too, if your heart is strong enough, would set off to, and live to tell about, the journey from the Mouth of Hell to the Mountain of the Moon.

Chapter 3
THE LITTLE MAN FROM THE
SIGNAGE DEPARTMENT

I was introduced to the Little Man from the Signage Department in a very informal way. I haven't even actually met him in the flesh. However, I am absolutely convinced he is out there somewhere.

Our destination was Vigo, a northern ancient Spanish city. It was going to be a long ride and darkness was already falling, the last few sun rays flickering on and off in the distant horizon in an attempt to prolong the afternoon.

The freeway stretched ahead, unusually light traffic occupying the warm asphalt lanes. I was getting ready for a little nap in the back of the car, adjusting the head support to make my forty winks as comfortable as possible. All was well when I lost contact with the world and drifted off to the land of Z's.

I woke up to the sounds of grumbling and grunting. It came from the direction of the driver's seat. It was getting dark outside and evidently a few hours had passed while I was asleep. I could tell my father was irritated. I inquired as to the source of his agitation.

Apparently, we were lost. "Vigo" was no longer our beacon and we were heading toward downtown Porto instead. We had missed an exit somehow. After consulting the map for some time, a revised route was established and we were on our way. We would have to go through Porto and get back on the northbound highway later.

Night had arrived. The miniature signs, already hard to read due to their size, were even more unreadable in the dark. As we drove past them, our headlights' illumination would offer only a split second for us to discern the lettering.

A fork in the road crept up on us suddenly, the signs located in between the two prongs. One could hardly read them before one had to make a choice. Not only that, but the two white, outlined signs offering the information, were positioned one immediately above the other, their arrow-like ends pointing in opposite ways, confusing the eye and making it difficult to see which way one should go.

With a screech, the car came to a halt, almost climbing over the traffic island. We stopped directly in front of the signs, our headlights fixed squarely upon their black inscriptions. We had them cornered and trapped. They had nowhere to run. Leisurely we read what they said and with all the time in the world, determined which was the correct way.

It was at that point that my father and I concluded there was a Little Man in the Signage Department, whose sole job was to see how he could confuse innocent road travelers like us. I was certain that every time we lost our bearings, the Little Man would laugh mischievously and celebrate with a glass of wine. Every time we managed to find our way, he would get back to the drawing board to devise a better scheme.

In this chapter, I will try to outline the Little Man's modus operandi, in the hope that this information will come in handy one day and save my readers from his waggish tricks.

The Little Man often strikes at the least convenient moment. In a way, he is a Murphy's Law representative on the Portuguese roadways, working relentlessly to foil the plans of journeyers and travelers.

If one fancies to plan a trip with mathematical precision, calculating departure, travel and arrival times, chances are the Little Man will find a way to derail the operation. If one gets directions to some location, it is likely that some sign somewhere will somehow manage to confuse one on one's way there.

I distinctly remember how a perfectly calm scene turned into a frantic rush one fine morning, as a result of the Little Man's pranks.

My father had a meeting in Amadora, a suburb of Lisbon, and asked me to come along. I had nothing better to do that morning so I joined him. We were halfway there and had plenty of time to arrive on time.

Not in a hurry in any fashion, our car was progressing down the northbound highway. The road was packed with automobiles, the traffic's condition somewhere between congestion and the sniffles. Our exit was supposed to be coming up shortly.

Chatting about the agenda of the meeting and the possible issues that might come up, we were less than attentive as to what was occurring around us. Suddenly, the traffic started moving faster, as if the freeway had just taken a sinus medicine.

In an attempt to catch up with the traffic, we accelerated along the left lane, cars still surrounding us.

"What did that sign say?" My father nearly leaped from his seat.

"Which one?" I asked, bewildered.

The sign was located on the far right side of the road, hidden behind the cars beside us. My father had a quick sight of it as we were passing by, but couldn't make out what it said.

Feeling a little anxious, unsure if we had missed our exit or not, we drove in silence for some time. Fifteen minutes later, having reached the inevitable conclusion we had indeed missed it, we turned about and got started in the opposite direction. We drove slower on the way back, keeping to the right, and careful not to miss our exit again. We had perhaps ten minutes to get to our meeting

Nervousness and frustration gradually replaced our anxiety. The traffic was sluggish, progressing only a few hundred meters a minute. I had a distinct feeling the Little Man was watching us from his office, smirking with joy. His secretary was preparing the wine and the lobster, and he was clearing his desktop to make room for the feast.

Time was ticking by and we were minutes away from being late. My father was wincing with irritation. The Little Man was licking his lips while the red lobster was loaded onto his plate and the wine bottle was being uncorked.

My gaze fell for a fraction of a second on a small road sign. It was positioned on the far right side, not higher than knee-level, where no one could see it. I managed to read the first few letters "Ama..." It disappeared immediately behind the other vehicles.

"It's right there!" I cried frantically, my finger pointed at the exit. It was the only sign heralding that exit, utterly unnoticeable to the unwary motorist.

The car thrust forward and then swerved to the right, cutting in front of the other cars. We made it onto the exit just as the Little Man was about to take his first bite of lobster. He was definitely disappointed.

So sure he was of his success that he hadn't bothered setting up any other traps for us on the way to our destination, and we arrived only ten minutes late. The Little Man was furious. His secretary came in and snatched the lobster and wine away as he reluctantly went back to the drawing board. It was my turn to make a toast.

But when it comes to contriving misleading signs,

the Little Man is a guru. Following Korzybski's philosophy that everything has two meanings, our friend from the Signage Department has created his own dogma: Every sign should be as vague as possible to allow for many interpretations.

One of his favorite ploys involves signs around traffic circles. A lonely arrow placed along the encircling road, pointing to an indeterminable course, can wreak untold havoc. At times it means one should turn at the next outlet and sometimes it means to keep going along the roundabout.

Placing signs in unusual spots is also a standard item in his bag of tricks.

I distinctly recall a time when I was following the blue signs leading to the Lisbon highway. I passed a "Lisbon" freeway sign pointing straight ahead. Half a block later, out of the corner of my eye I caught a glimpse of an inconspicuous sign attached to a lamppost on the right-hand corner of the street, indicating the way to the freeway was rightwards. Had I not noticed it, I would have carried on forward, probably till I arrived in Porto.

Once, coming back from a meeting near the Lisbon International airport, I sought the *auto-estrada* to Cascais. I passed through several intersections in search of blue highway signs and eventually found one. I followed its course only to find myself driving down a road under construction, heading downtown, with no further blue signs to follow.

Well, if his tricks had stopped at that, I would be quite thankful. Alas, his cunning mind never ceased to invent new ways of deceiving the unadvised travelers.

Bored with road signs which gave, or in his case omitted, information on where one was going, the Little Man from the Signage Department decided to try his luck in traffic signs. Stop signs, no parking signs, no-entry signs and others of this sort provided a new and unexplored avenue to expand his sphere of influence.

I recall one late night when I was returning from an exciting night in Lisbon. There were hardly any cars around and the roads were deserted. Heading home, I decided to try a different route home. Coming around a bend, I was suddenly faced with a no-go sign, which stood on a traffic island where the road branched off into two different streets.

I came to a mad halt, confused at what I should do. The sign gave no indication as to which of the two roads ahead was the one-way street, and since there were no other vehicles roaming about, I had no means of finding out. I waited there for some time, hoping inspiration would somehow come to me. But it never did. I ended up following the right-hand lane and eventually arrived home safely, thanking heaven for protecting me and my Fiat.

Such new contrivances, however, always resolved if one used one's head long enough. In my case, the no-go signal must have applied to the left road. And here is the explanation which flashed through my mind belatedly. (If you manage to understand it, pour yourself a glass of wine for your first victory over the Little Man.)

Suppose the no-go sign was intended for the lane at the right. My only way would be leftwards. The oncoming traffic would be arriving from the right and would have to cross my lane. In that case, a stop sign, a traffic light or a give-way stripe would be in order and there were none. QED the one-way sign referred to the left-hand prong.   Simple, is it not?

Another example exists right across the street from my apartment. In this intersection, there is a one way street climbing up the hill and another two-way street going across it. In the entire intersection there is only one stop sign to those coming along the two-way street from the right. There are no other traffic signs. The locals solve it by honking their horns before driving through the intersection. It works.

In summary, the best policy to follow in resolving riddles imposed upon you by confusing signs is to stop at the side of the road with ample warning to other drivers, and quietly work out the puzzle. Or ask someone for directions (N.B. I strongly advise the reader to have studied chapter five before asking any Portuguese for directions.)

Ninety nine percent of the time these riddles are the work of the Little Man from the Signage Department, in which case there is a logical way out. For the remaining one percent, there is no solution. It is just an error committed by the Little Man's *colega* and in that case, I wish you luck.

Surprisingly, the Little Man from the Signage Department is also a man of good merits.

In a way, he is quite essential to the life in Portugal. In the fast-paced and giddy world of Portuguese transportation, someone has to make the speed devils slow down occasionally.

And that is where our friend enters the scene. From his lofty office, masterminding the shrewdest placement and displacement of highway and traffic signs executed by his minions and accomplices under the wings of the night while the unsuspecting citizens of Portugal are fast asleep, he takes on the role of an invisible police officer.

It is a simple proposition. If one wants to know where one is headed, one has to decelerate in order to read those specially designed signs.

To illustrate this concept, here is a living and breathing example of his cunning speed traps at work.

I was going to pick up my friend Teresa from her home in Queluz, near Lisbon. We were going to see a movie, and I was running a little late. My little Fiat was doing its best to go faster, but the real problem was that I had left too late. As you can see, I was getting into the Portuguese spirit.

I was almost there when I reached the trap in the form of a wide traffic circle. The large sign showed a drawing with four roads leading away from the roundabout, much like a clock with exits marked on the twelfth, third, sixth, and ninth hours. I was coming from the six o'clock mark.

The sign was placed very close to the circle and since I was driving as fast as my Fiat would go (it wasn't very fast), I only had a second to glance at it. Nevertheless, I had managed to observe that my exit was located on the twelve o'clock mark. I felt victorious -- the Little Man had failed in confusing me. I had outwitted him.

I swerved rapidly into the turnabout, avoiding collision with a large bus, and was getting ready to rush for my exit. And then it hit me. I realized there were only two other outlets from the roundabout, and these were on the two and ten o'clock marks! Which one was I to follow? I had to slow down and decide what to do.

I took the ten o'clock exit. It was the wrong one, of course. I gritted my teeth in frustration. Here I was, running late, going up the wrong road and surrounded by traffic. I made a U-turn and drove back to the roundabout. An identical sign welcomed me and again I looked in vain for the fourth exit. It didn't exist.

There was only one other choice and it proved to be the correct one. I raced around and got to her address. When she got in the car, I at once told her how the Little Man had successfully fooled me. She giggled, saying her sister never complained of problems with the traffic signs. I protested: maybe her sister did have difficulties with the signs but never voiced them?

To prove my point, I drove back through that same roundabout. Again, the familiar sign welcomed us, and I could have sworn it was chuckling sadistically as we were approaching.

"There you are, the sign shows four exits while in actual fact, there are only three!" I said triumphantly.

"But what about that one over there?" She was pointing at a little path to a school, at the seven o'clock position, which seemed more like a bike trail than a road.

"That couldn't be it," I argued.

"It is too," she asserted defensively. "That is the exit to the school, which the sign indicates as the fourth exit."

"But it is not anywhere close to the position the sign showed. It is almost connected to the main road," I said meekly, defeated once again.

"You just have to pay closer attention," was the reassuring and encouraging reply.

The fourth exit wasn't where it was supposed to be, and it didn't look like an exit either. But it was indeed there. Next time I would decelerate and be on the alert when approaching a roundabout, I promised myself. Deep in the vaults of the Signage Department, the Little Man was cheerfully uncorking a bottle of vintage wine, celebrating a double victory. Not only had he outsmarted me, but also taught me a lesson.

By now, after reading all of my horror stories, you must be having second thoughts about motoring in Portugal. I must therefore end with the statement that a positive side does exist to all of this which makes all the trouble you will ever encounter with signs, worth its while.

The other virtue of the Little Man lies with his inclination toward the preservation of nature. Although playful, this man is not an evil man. He may adore trickery and love the everlasting challenge of who would outsmart whom. Above all, he might do everything within his power to win at it and thus satisfy his large appetite for lobsters and the never-quenching thirst for wine. But he would never dream of hurting anybody or anything.

Thus, to remove bushes or root out trees in order to hang his signs would never cross his mind. To spoil the beauty of nature with large and tasteless signs would never be his deed.

That is why the signs in Portugal are small and tend to blend in with the environment. One often finds signs hidden behind trees, covered by overgrown bushes and concealed amongst flowerbeds.

And that is also the reason why signs are not abundant in this country. The infrequency of signs allows the spectator to view Mother Nature in an unadulterated fashion. Even the signs along the highways are often too small.

What a song it is to drive along a country road without the modern signs constantly pestering you with announcements you don't care to read.

So while we might complain about him and his practical jokes, deep inside we always appreciate the existence of our good friend in the Signage Department, whose contribution to a lovely and untamed country is cherished in our hearts.

Chapter 4
WINDMILLS, CATS AND
MAGIC POTIONS

I first heard of it on the grapevine. A windmill, over a hundred and fifty years old, restored to its original condition, was operating on the weekends somewhere near Peniche, where one could taste bread from freshly ground wheat. Enchanted by the idea, I was determined to explore this legend first-hand.

We arrived in Torres Vedras on Saturday morning. It was a town, about fifty kilometers north of Lisbon, located near the Sizandro River. When asking for directions, the repeated response was, "Oh, the windmill!" followed by an excited explanation of the way there.

It wasn't too difficult to find. Standing there on the left-hand side of the road, three stories high and perhaps thirty feet in diameter, magnificently and unusually shaped, it was truly an object out of place and time. Although I had never been in a real windmill before, an inexplicable yet distinct feeling I had been there and done that, came over me.

I was standing in front of this ancient and humble structure, absorbing the view, determined not to miss any detail. The white circular tower was defined at its top and bottom by a slightly thicker, azure layer of brick, forming a sort of a ring at each end. The sky-blue layer extended up and down from the lower and higher rings, following the outlines of the doorway and the windows and creating an intriguingly simple design. The chipped paint, especially around the doorframe, revealing the tan brick layer underneath, added the semblance of age and antiquity to the otherwise restored edifice.

The tar-covered, conoid roof with its thin, iron rooster fixed at its tip telling the direction of the wind, served as the lid for the giant cylinder. The eight huge wooden masts, only two of which were carrying a sail, were slowly turning in the wind, almost touching the floor as they whooshed by.

I entered through the small doorway and found myself in between the first and second floor, the former being below ground level. I lowered my head to peek under the wooden platform, the first floor ceiling, which was at my shoulders' height. The room had an old rickety table, several chairs, an outdated black telephone hanging on the far wall and a thick wooden pillar supporting the ceiling.

Cobwebs decorated each vacant nook and cranny and I wondered just how many little spiders inhabited the place. Or maybe, I shuddered at the thought, there was only one of them, a really big and busy one.

At the table, sat an old man. He slowly got up to

his feet to greet me, a pleasant smile across his face. He was neatly and tastefully dressed with a pair of tan slacks, a darker light-knitted pullover, and a matching tan cap.

He introduced himself as Armando dos Santos and said he was appointed by the village to be the custodian of the windmill when it was recently renovated, since he was one of the few experts on windmills in Portugal. He had been in the business non-stop since he was twelve, when his grandfather put him to work in the family's windmill. *Senhor* Santos had his own restored windmill (which was over two hundred and seventy years old,) located right next to his house, where he worked whenever not at the village.

Chuckling at the memory, he recounted a time when one fine day a few years back, a couple from Luxembourg pulled up in front of his windmill, driving an elegant Mercedes, an interpreter occupying the back seat. They wanted to see if the windmill was fully operational, which it was -- Santos cared for it as a father looked after his child.

Then, after inspecting it and hearing a bit of the windmill's history, the man asked *Senhor* Santos how much he wanted for it. He responded without a second thought that the man hadn't enough money to buy it.

The man from Luxembourg furiously demanded to know how could *Senhor* Santos possibly know how much money he had. Santos calmly responded that simply put, no amount of money in the world could ever buy his windmill as it wasn't for sale. The man from Luxembourg turned around, his face red with anger, and left without another word, pulling his wife by the hand back to the car, the interpreter hurrying behind to catch up with them.

Senhor Santos paused for a moment, thinking. Then he added with some regret that he thought he could have been more polite to that man. I was astonished. Santos didn't care about the fact that he could have received several millions for his windmill. He was not going to weep about missing that opportunity.

Here was a man who valued his little treasure more than any amount of money in the world. Not only was it a treasure but it gave him a sense of satisfaction and accomplishment. Unlike some people, for him there were exceptions to the "everything has a price" rule. What was the use of receiving wads of cash if one had to part with his source of happiness and pride in life? In our rapidly progressing world, where modernization raced ahead of human relations, it was refreshing to find someone who had still maintained his values and integrity.

One might say that once Santos would have gotten the money he would have been happier and able to lead an easier life but as it was he looked twenty years younger than his seventy-seven years. He moved about agilely, handled heavy bags of grain and wheat on a daily basis, as well as toured visitors through the windmill. He was clearheaded and smiled often. No amount of money could ever pay for that sort of happiness and health, because such commodities just can't be bought.

Well, one story often leads to another and as I

love little anecdotes, I didn't stop him. Several years ago the mast in his windmill was in need of repair. He called in the specialist from the village. When the young man disassembled the massive parts, he found an aged note hidden between two adjoining pieces of wood. It was a letter from the young man's grandfather, written forty-seven years ago.   His grandfather had also been a wood specialist in his time and unbeknownst to his grandson, was the one who restored the windmill for Santos half a century before. *Senhor* Santos' eyes turned misty at the memory.

The note was addressed to whoever came to fix the mill in the future, stating that this was the grandfather's last work as he was retiring, and expressing a hope that his work was done well and would last for many years to come. Such were the dedication and pride of the men years ago, I reflected with awe, pondering this touching tale.

My musing was rudely interrupted by a black cat with white patches around its head, tail and paws, which strolled in as if it owned the place. *Senhor* Santos introduced it as the windmill's companion. Every windmill had a cat which kept it free of birds and mice, just as the spiders kept it free of insects and bugs. The feline would enter and leave as it wished through a six-inch wide hole in the lower right corner of the door, but usually stayed away in strong winds, due to the excessive noise. This one did a good job of safeguarding the mill, Santos affirmed, petting it on the head affectionately.

I asked him why the windmill was positioned in the center of the village. Wouldn't the houses interfere with the wind blowing at the mill? My question stirred quite a reaction. Frowning and shaking his head, *Senhor* Santos said the windmill had been there before any of the village buildings were erected. Yet they built and built and built, in front of the windmill, near it and behind it, as if it had to be sheltered from the wind. He sneered at the idea. To make matters worse, he added, the weather has been changing over the last few years.

Wait a minute, I stopped him. What exactly did he mean by that statement? He let out a deep sigh and with an unfocused gaze, returned to his childhood. Back then, the wind blew strong and steady. The weather was predictable. Each morning, one could tell the forecast for the day.

Nowadays, he said glumly, the weather was unreliable. The wind changed often and it was getting more and more difficult to predict what it would do a few hours later, making the windmill operator's job much harder. With the pollution, the massive cutting down of forests and with little regard to the environment, Man was changing nature in a drastic way, the full consequences of which not yet realized.

After a long and thoughtful pause, he motioned for me to follow him up to the top floor. The narrow staircase, not wider than a foot, spiraled up along the circular wall all the way to the third floor.   I looked around in amazement.

The roof supports hung low at head level and the

large wooden beam (also called a mast) which was connected to the rig outside, spanned diagonally across to the other side of the room, leaving just enough room to pass under it. A huge cogwheel was mounted vertically around the mast, its "teeth" facing ahead. A smaller, wooden wheel with a few thick short poles was positioned in front of the bigger cogwheel, the large teeth fitting in between the poles. The smaller wheel was mounted onto a thick shaft which in turn was connected to the top millstone.

Senhor Santos passed his hand over the millstones' wooden cover affectionately, as if it was a living and breathing thing. As the wind blows on the sails outside, he explained, the mast is turned, rotating the millstone through the cogwheels and shaft mechanism. The large cogwheel has thirty-two teeth, "like we do," and the small one has either seven or eight poles. If any other number of teeth or poles were used, the windmill would not work.

The stones were made by hand, their crafters chiseling away at them for months before achieving the shape and texture required of a millstone. A stone would last for sixty years usually, grinding for twelve hours a day, every day of the year.

Tiny whitish specks created an almost imperceptible film of flour covering the walls and the wooden beams, and now *Senhor* Santos' hand. As he rested his arm on his waist, the white powder transferred to his pullover, clinging onto the fabric. *Senhor* Santos was beaming, I observed. That was where he was most happy -- up in the top floor of a windmill, where the noise and clatter formed a smooth rhythm and getting covered with flour was part of one's job.

Whereas I tried to avoid touching the whitish dust, Santos seemed to intentionally lean on those objects which were covered the most. It looked as if he actually enjoyed feeling the existence of the flour around him. After all, flour meant survival, work and a fully stocked kitchen.

He solemnly went on to explain the way the mill mechanism worked and the importance of operating it correctly. Underneath the millstones' cover, the lower stone always remained stationary. A lever fixed in the floor -- he reverently bent down and patted it -- could lower or raise the top millstone's position, monitoring how much space was between the two stones. The smaller the gap, the finer the flour would be. If the gap was too small and too many grains fell into the hole, the entire windmill, mast and all, could stop and even break down.

Which led to the next subject. The wheat was held in a rectangular container with a slightly sloped pan at its end. The pan was connected to a wooden stick which, much like a vinyl record player's needle, was resting on the stone. The faster the "record" would turn the more the pan would be vibrated by the "needle" and the more wheat would drop into the grinding space.

In what *Senhor* Santos termed moderate winds --when the millstone completed a turn two to three times a second -- the mill would produce approximately sixty kilos of flour in one day. In strong winds -- I got dizzy when I heard it, the millstone turns around sixty to seventy times a second -- fifty to sixty kilos of flour get produced in one hour.

At the side of the millstones' cover there was an opening through which the ground wheat came out into a large receptacle. The opening was covered by a cloth to prevent the wind from blowing the flour away.

And now, Santos said with a mischievous smile, his pullover patched white, the sailing lessons begin.

Sailing? Where was the boat? I asked.

Santos' expression indicated he was slightly offended. Why, we were in it! Without waiting a second longer, he reached for a wooden wheel with long handles, which was fixed to the roof directly under the point where the mast came in.

I was staring in amazement, my mouth open. Not only had I missed that helm-like object's existence, but also I was entirely baffled by its purpose.

With expert deftness, "Captain" Santos untied the thick white rope which was around the helm. Having slackened the rope, he was thus able to remove the pulley at its other end from a metal ring protruding from the wall. I looked around in amazement. There was a ring every four feet or so all around the room, which again I had not noticed. By then I was convinced a visit to an optician was in order.

Giving it more rope, he hooked the pulley to the next ring. His hands moved faster than I could follow, and within seconds the rope was taut all around, its end tied to the wheel. He pointed up to an iron arrow which was hanging from the tip of the roof. It was connected to the rooster outside, I realized. It showed those inside which way the wind blew.

With a smile on his face, he went ahead and began turning the helm.

I stared as the entire roof, mast and rig included, began rotating to the right! He kept spinning the wheel, the pulley and rope creaking and sighing under the heavy load. When the mast was aligned with the arrow up above, he quickly secured the wheel at that position using another rope. He wiped off a few beads of sweat that had appeared on his forehead, coloring it white in the process.

So, that was how one sailed a windmill! Being a sailor myself for many years, I couldn't resist the challenge. I begged him to let me try it.

He willingly released the steering wheel from its position and let me be at the helm. I peeked up around the mast to observe the arrow above us. The wind had changed in the meantime and our course was now a few degrees off. I held onto the wooden grips and pulled down with all my might. It was hard, but it did move. I managed with some effort to get the mast aligned with the arrow and proudly secured the helm.   I was on my way to becoming a windmill operator, I was assured.

The roof, he explained, had a set of wooden wheels under it. There was a tiny wheel every two feet or so, with more wheels directly under the mast. The roof with the attached rig weighed more than five tons. I gasped, realizing I had just moved the weight of three elephants. And what if one of the wheels broke, I wondered to myself.

Santos indicated a small rectangular recess below the track, as if reading my mind. This was where one could take out old wheels and put in new ones as needed. By moving the roof over to the position where the bad wheel was directly above the "pit," one could then undo the axle and the wheel would simply drop down into one's hand. The new wheel goes up through the chute into its position, gets secured with the iron axle and Voila! it works like new.

One last thing we mustn't forget was to secure the roof, now that it had a new position. On each side, there was a thick line wrapped around the roof supports, with a hook at its end. These were quickly fastened to the nearest metal ring and tightened. In extremely strong winds, I was informed, the entire top could be blown off.

The ropes, he mentioned, were over three hundred years old, given to him by a friend who received it from his grandfather's grandfather. They were thick and bulky, but they outlived many new ropes, like the ones that were originally in the windmill when Santos bought it -- these became useless after a few years.

Stooping over the end product, the heap of freshly ground flour in its large receptacle, *Senhor* Santos cogitated for a minute or two. If one was stupid and ignorant, he said finally, one would now use the sieve to rid it of the wheat shells.

Reading the huge question mark on my face, he

went on to clarify. The shells contain a large portion of the important nutrients in wheat. To discard the shells is to rid of much of the bread's dietary riches. Thus white bread was very low in nutrients compared with whole-wheat bread.

Senhor Santos also mentioned that ever since he was a little child, his mother fed him a magic potion every morning. The elixir was composed of three spoons of properly ground whole wheat mixed in with a glass of milk. He had never stopped eating it either -- that had been his breakfast for the last seventy-plus years. And, to point out its effectiveness, though humble at that, he remarked that he was in excellent shape. And I couldn't agree more. I bought a kilo on the spot.

In reality, he whispered, it wasn't only the consumption of the magic potion every morning which made him feel and look as young as he did. Keeping himself busy every day, working at the windmill, was a major factor as well. One can't do nothing all day and expect to stay young, he said.   So true, I thought. I recalled attending a gastronomic party in Sintra where I met an eighty-six year old man who played the guitar and sang *fado* songs for all the guests. Not only could he play the guitar, but he would work many hours each day at his garden, our party host asserted. Each time he would go and visit the elder, he found him working diligently outside, sleeves rolled up. The old man was, to put it mildly, healthy and strong.

I gave the room one last look before following *Senhor* Santos to the second floor, the cat bouncing down the stairs ahead of us. There I found a similar set-up to the one I had just studied, only this one was solely used to grind corn. Wheat and corn, I found out, had to be ground separately as different millstones were used in each process.

The tour concluded with a visit to the café. It was located next to the windmill, and the smell of fresh bread was in the air. Following my nostrils, I arrived at the entrance and ordered some bread at once. One woman was molding the flour into loaves and putting them into the traditional wood-burning oven while the other was taking the baked ones out and putting them in paper bags to keep them warm.

The bread proved to be delicious. It was warm, fresh and to my amazement, was full of flavor. I was surprised to find myself satisfied after several bites, a fact which I attributed to the extremely high number of nutrients in each slice.

Sitting there, a kilo of magic powder for the youth potion in my possession, drinking a *carioca de limão* and casually nibbling on the natural bread, I found myself feeling unusually happy and cheerful. *Senhor* Santos' passion for the profession, his friendly demeanor, hospitality and cheerfulness, as well as his companions -- the windmill, the cat and the magic potion -- had inspired me forever in a way I would never forget.

Chapter 5
BEYOND FIRST IMPRESSIONS

If I had paid attention solely to my first impressions of Portugal, I couldn't have possibly enjoyed myself there as much as I did.

The Portuguese people are usually an amicable and cheerful people. However most of them don't like to hurry. Customers are not always at the top of the list, especially if the waitress' boyfriend is on the phone or if an important soccer match is being shown live on television.

As a result, we, the customers, can get rather irritated. What about some service, we demand. But our grunts and grumbles are ignored. We might leave Portugal with a distinct feeling of irritation and with the conclusion that the Portuguese are very rude and impolite. I nearly reached that very wrong conclusion myself.

Politeness in a large way depends on the customs of the people involved. As an example, this used to be a serious barrier in business meetings between Americans and Japanese. What was the proper way to address a Japanese executive, by his first surname, his second one or both? Did you shake hands or bow in greeting? Since the culture of the East was vastly different than that of the West, we were aware of the existence of a wide abyss between the two and attempted to put an effort toward building a bridge across it.

In Portugal such an abyss does exist, often unbeknownst to the foreigner. Portugal is considered to be part of Europe, however its people don't always follow the same rules of conduct.

What would you do if upon reaching a specific store that had been recommended, you find it closed with a "*Volto ja*" sign on display while the owner was drinking a coffee around the corner? Possibly vow to never shop there again. What would you say if the waiter talked on the phone for ten minutes before coming and giving you the menu? Probably leave the restaurant or ask for the manager. When I first arrived in Portugal, I was inclined to do the same.

However, for the majority of the Portuguese, this is normal. A ten-minute wait for the menu at a restaurant is acceptable. Nobody is in a rush anyway.

Lateness is often dismissed without a frown. The people are lenient and easy-going. Life is not so harsh.

"So he is late. Probably there was a traffic jam, or maybe he couldn't find his way easily, or perhaps he met a friend in the street he hadn't seen in ten years," says the person who is waiting, and takes this opportunity to drink another coffee.

As odd as it may sound, beyond that negative first impression lies a country whose golden hearted inhabitants are keen on helping their fellows. In all my travels around Portugal, the number of people who rendered unsympathetic and cold service could be counted on one hand. The hundreds of others have been more than helpful in every way.

A small anecdote would be in order.

I was at a gas station somewhere in the Alentejo one afternoon, filling up my Fiat's tank. All the while, I was observing a man trying to get the water pump to function so he could wash his van's windshield, without much success. From the license plate, I gathered he was from Germany. The attendant was close by, talking to a few friends. The man soon gave up and stood by his van, waiting for the attendant to come over and assist him. He even waved a few times in vain, trying to attract some attention.

I finally walked over to the German and told him to go and talk to the attendant, which he did.

"Oh, the attendant is over at the diesel pump," said the man we mistook for an attendant, and pointed to the other side of the station. "I am waiting for him as well." The German went over there and the attendant helped him at once by showing him the location of another water pump that was operational. The German successfully cleaned the windshield and drove off happily.

Deeply involved in assisting only one customer, the attendant wasn't aware of the existence of other people. But once his attention was drawn to it, he immediately assisted the other client in a very cordial and earnest way.

Not knowing how the Portuguese behaved, the German might have just got in his car and driven off in frustration. Or worse, he could have started raising his voice at the attendant, which would have achieved absolutely nothing. So a foreigner's first impression of the Portuguese could easily be that of rudeness and inefficiency.

In restaurants, **paying** for the meal is sometimes a ridiculously long process. One has to first get the waiter's attention to ask for the bill, since he will never "happen to be around" when the payment time comes along, as they do in some other countries.

Then it might take a while to get the bill put together. It finally arrives, always on top of a plate or inside a cover of sorts, and the waiter leaves the area again, giving one ample time to look it over. Now one has to find the waiter again, which might take some more time. He shows up eventually and one receives the change shortly after with a large friendly smile.

The waiter is not trying to irritate one. He doesn't hate foreigners either. He simply takes his time about doing things, all the while being very polite by not hanging over your shoulder while the last bite of your dessert is being consumed or appearing to be anxious to be paid.

The Portuguese's urge to help is very evident when one asks for directions.

Inevitably, when one asks for information about getting to a specific location, the person will make every effort to help you, even if he doesn't know the way. In most cases it troubles them greatly that they can't assist you, and so they will explain where you can find someone that can.

One instance that springs to mind was when I was on my way to a suburb of Lisbon that was under extensive road construction. Stopping by a shopping center, I asked a man walking his dog how to get to my destination.

The fellow spent a few minutes in deep thought, adjusting his tie with his free hand. Then, not being able to remember how to get there, he explained how the numerous detours were so confusing and apologized for not knowing the way.

I was about to thank him and drive off when he told me to wait. He then began looking around for someone else who might know the way. Not finding anyone right there, he disappeared into the shopping center lobby with his dog!

A moment later he returned saying the receptionist was busy on the phone but would surely know how to get there. I was stunned at how far a complete stranger would go in an effort to assist me with directions. I thanked him profusely and followed his advice.

Now, this deed may seem stupid to some but that's what I call unselfish.

Once I lost my way to a friend's place where he

was having his birthday party. I stopped by two pedestrians and asked for the way to his street. The taller of the two started at once to describe how to get there, when suddenly the other one cut him off and said it was all wrong. He knew the right way, and went on to explain.

I waited there for a few minutes while they argued. Finally, they asked a lady that was walking by to arbitrate. There was hope, I thought innocently. The woman heard their stories and then solemnly went on to impart her own version of the way there, which was entirely different.

I watched in alarm as they all started to discuss the matter. I turned off the engine and sat there bewildered, the small but loud conference becoming a matter of interest for other passerbys. Luckily, none joined in and about five minutes later the original council reached what seemed to be an agreed upon route, which they excitedly relayed to me. I thanked all three with deep gratitude and they each went their way merrily.

The odd Portuguese habit of repeating the directions several times over may seem puzzling initially and even absurd. Almost every person I have asked for assistance in finding my way, unless he or she was extremely busy, repeated his instructions several times over.

This routine has two purposes.

First of which is to ensure the lost sheep (me) really understands the descriptions of the right route. If the shepherd repeats it several times there is a better chance of comprehension at the other end. And the reasons for the shepherd's justified fear that his sheep will be lost again, are the existence of the Little Man and his confusing signs as well as the usual intricacy of the Portuguese road systems.

For example, I have frequently heard the phrase *"sempre em frente,"* which means straight ahead. Well, this phrase, often used in giving directions, is more of an expression than an instruction to be taken literally. The meaning of "don't take any turns" is more accurate.

I recall one time when I have been told to continue *sempre em frente* and followed the straight narrow road. All was fine and dandy but then a hundred meters later the road widened and curved leftward. I was no longer going forward but to the left. The road then reached a roundabout with two other exits. Which one was the continuation of my street? The only solution was to locate another shepherd, as the sheep was lost again.

So *sempre em frente* should be regarded with caution and followed wisely, if only from the standpoint that in Portugal there isn't a single street that goes absolutely straight ahead. It is just a fact of life. Having been told to go *sempre em frente* I drive along the street to my best ability, never taking any turns, and ask for new directions at the first moment a difficulty arises, such as the appearance of a roundabout or a fork in the road.

And so the shepherds, knowing these peculiarities, attempt to compensate for the obstacles by repeating their directions. Sometimes the instructions are repeated in different versions to overcome these barriers. The following dialogue is typical:

"Straight ahead then a left turn followed by a right turn after the school," says the shepherd.

I nod with understanding.

"So you simply go forward, turn left and then you will see the school. Take the next right turn," comes a second set of instructions that seems to be the sequel to the first one.

"After following the road straight for two hundred meters, turn left and once you pass the school turn right," is the final set.

It takes time to realize that all three sets are in fact one and the same, just repeated differently. However, having been given three versions of the same set of instructions, there is less of a chance that one would lose one's way again.

The second purpose of repeating the instructions is to prolong the conversation. The majority of the Portuguese simply love to talk, and every opportunity to engage in a discussion is pounced upon.

Now, you may ask how many times does one need to ask for directions. Well, during my first month in Portugal, I usually spent more time asking for directions than driving.

Thus this forced encounter which ordinarily is highly impersonal across the globe, had been turned by the people of Portugal into a social and friendly affair, where they get a chance to display their manners and willingness to help as well as enjoy talking to strangers.

Time and again I have seen the person whom I approached for directions regard the task as a personal crusade and immediately take me under his wings. As a rule, people will not relay the directions to you from a distance or in a hasty manner. They will stop whatever they have been doing and draw nearer to discuss the issue.

I once asked a man if he knew where a certain street was. He at once felt obliged to assist me. But first he signaled for me to pull into a taxi parking spot ten yards away and followed me there. Never mind the fact that it was in the opposite direction of where he was heading a moment ago, or that there wasn't even much traffic on the road. Giving directions was a serious matter and required the lost sheep's undivided attention.

He paused for a minute in deep thought and then explained to me in great detail how to get there. The way there was quite complicated but I eventually managed to understand it after he had repeated it in different versions. I could actually sense his joy of having been able to assist me.

"*Muito obrigado*," I thanked him heartily at the end.

"*De nada*," he replied beaming, and went off on his way cheerfully.

The other habit is to provide several sets of directions, each representing a distinctly separate way of getting there. This way, one can have freedom of choice about how to get to one's destination. For example, if there was a longer way that usually had less traffic and was faster, it would be offered as well. Or perhaps one of the two routes requires paying toll while the other one doesn't. Be sure that they will tell you about it.

And to give the finishing touches to my point, I must confess that this desire to help is contagious. One day I had to pull over close to *Boca do Inferno,* as my cellular phone was ringing. Once I hung up, a man approached me from the other side of the road asking for directions to Parede, a town east of Cascais.

Without a thought, I took my seat belt off and immediately got out of the car. I then explained to him in great detail how he should drive *sempre em frente* till the large roundabout, then take the second exit and go *sempre em frente* from there. I energetically repeated it a few times to make sure he really got it.

He thanked me profusely and drove off while I returned cheerfully back to my car. The lost sheep had become the shepherd, I reflected with amusement.

When I first arrived in Portugal the excessive number of dogs and cats in the streets fascinated me. This fact had been drawn to my attention as an unpleasant surprise one day, as I was stepping out of my car. I was about to lock the door when a small dog wearing no collar or identification walked by, lifted his leg over my front tire and carried on his way as if nothing had happened.

My great liking for the canine race didn't prevent me from feeling slightly offended. After all, my car had just been marked as a dog's property. Although I came to forget about that incident, I haven't been able to ignore ever since the multitude of dogs running around the streets.

I have noticed them dogtrotting around in packs, always seeming determined as if heading to a certain meeting in a specific location. Large Terriers teamed up with small Corggis. Spaniels mixed up with Poodle look-alikes. Groomed dogs with a collar paired with stray, shabby curs. The variation of sizes and colors were infinite. My first impression was that the Portuguese didn't take care of their best friends. How could there be so many poor dogs on the loose?

I saw a stray mongrel once, roaming past the restaurant where I was eating. I whistled at him, attempting to get him to come over. He didn't even look at me. I then threw a piece of bread in his path and he merely glanced at it, hopped over it without interest and carried on his way.

I was shocked. I have never seen a dog ignore food that was practically thrown at its feet. It was at that point that my curiosity was roused. The next dog ignored the bread and didn't even glance at it. I was resolute on getting to the bottom of this mystery.

A few days later, my first clue came into sight when I was having lunch at a chicken grill restaurant in main street Cascais. A bitch, perhaps a mixture of Collie and German Shepherd, was walking slowly along the tables. I called her and whistled at her many times in vain. One of the waiters was standing on the other side of the array of tables, chatting to a friend. The bitch went straight over and stood there by his feet.

The man petted her affectionately till the end of the conversation and then went inside while she remained in her place. A moment later, the waiter came back, a collection of leftovers on an aluminum foil in his hand. He walked to a corner away from the dining area and placed it on the floor for her. He stepped back, allowing her to commence dinner, but the bitch started walking away from it! My jaw nearly dropped to the floor. What was wrong with these dogs?

The man called her back and pointed at the food, telling her she better eat it after all the work it took to put the dinner together. He was actually talking to the dog, I noticed, a habit many Portuguese tend to indulge in. She eventually began eating, seemingly more out of duty than desire.

The next day, I noticed how another tiny mongrel at another restaurant was scouting the floor around the outside tables. The owner of the restaurant who was grilling the fish right there, threw a few worthless pieces toward him, which he consumed slowly.

And then it all made sense. The dogs were in fact taken care of to such an extent that hardly any canine creature walked around hungry. The dogs were left to their own devices and were treated more or less like humans, I realized. They ate at the neighborhood restaurants, traveled around together and were the real owners of the Portuguese roads.

Many of them would adopt a street and assume the title of neighborhood car chaser, which apparently bestowed many privileges upon the canine bearer. They bask in the sun, sprawled over the road completely oblivious of the traffic, forcing the drivers to pass around them. Honking at the honorary member of the nobility doesn't produce any effect, unless one is very persistent with the use of his horn. The dog might get up and move out of the way if you're lucky that day. Most often they just lift their heads, give you a "who are you?" look and fall back to sleep. Dogs in Portugal, I concluded, had a life of luxury.

    The final straw that broke my first impression's back had to do with a cat. I was sitting in the lounge of a posh five-star hotel, drinking a *carioca de limão* and gazing over the balcony at the ocean. The room was fancy and elaborately decorated, the aura of richness and splendor radiating all around. A row of tall half-open windows provided an imperceptible flow of air which kept the lounge cool.

    A couple sat in the spacious sofa on the far corner while a family occupied the cluster of chairs nearby. A few businessmen discussed important matters at the other far corner. The tall waiter, wearing a dark tuxedo suit, attended to everyone's needs.

    And then, from the corner of my eye I noticed a white cat walking along one of the windowsills. It came by the executive corner and they marveled at its appearance. It became the focus of attention for a moment. The cat majestically strode from there over to the family, where it found a cozy spot in the lap of the young daughter, who petted it with enthusiasm. After some time it traveled over to the couple across the way and parked beside the lady, who stroked its white fur absentmindedly.

After an hour of non-stop affection from the guests, it slipped away unnoticed through the window. It then struck me that the cat wasn't the hotel cat. It had no collar around its neck. It was merely a stray cat which dropped in to pay a visit, obviously known to the waiter and perhaps to the guests as well.

My final conclusion was that there was no better place for a member of the canine or feline families to reside than in Portugal.

Another first impression which went by the boards rather quickly, concerned the *bombeiros voluntários* of Portugal, the fire fighters of each city, town and village in Portugal

When one travels through Portugal, one undoubtedly notices the various cars, trucks and ambulances that carry the *bombeiros voluntários* emblem. The vehicles are never uniform and at times even differ in color. With the array of Citroens, Mercedes vans, Renaults and other car makes, some painted red and some blue, my first impression was that the fire department was unprofessional and disorganized.

I was quite surprised, however, when Mr. Rama da Silva gave me an extensive tour of the Cascais fire station and told me about the history and tradition of the *bombeiros voluntários*. To my astonishment, out of the 43,000 fire fighters in the country, only perhaps three thousand are paid full-time employees. The rest are all volunteers.

Yes, volunteers. They all have regular jobs and work at the *bombeiros* station on their free time. I pondered over this concept for a while in amazement. What motivates people to daily put their lives on the line on a voluntary basis and without at least some monetary compensation?

Perhaps the answer might be found in its tradition. The concept was born over six hundred years ago, in the city of Lisbon. Seamen and fishermen, proficient in putting out fires while at sea, were asked to assist in putting out fires around the commercial areas at a time when no institution was in existence to deal with such catastrophes. Since that time, the population took it upon themselves to take care of fires around the country. Associations have been formed over the years and currently there are over seven hundred of them operating around Portugal. Each village and town has its own *bombeiros voluntários* unit which is composed of volunteers from that town or village.

Long ago the function of paramedic services was adopted by many *bombeiros* units. In coastal areas the function of sea rescue was included as well, while in rural areas the fields and forests were divided up and assigned to the appropriate *bombeiros* unit. Currently, about ninety percent of all rescue operations across the country are carried by out the *bombeiros voluntários*.

The *bombeiros* units accept donations as well as services from the local people. Therefore many businesses and individuals donate time and money to the *bombeiros*. A group of hotels in Cascais take turns feeding the fire fighters whenever there is a fire. The chief calls up the hotel whose turn it is, inform them of how many *bombeiros* are on the scene and the hotel prepares food for that many people and transports it out there. Companies allow workers who are *bombeiros* to slip away in times of need.

In that respect it is an organization of the people for the people, funded and supported by the people. Perhaps they don't have the most advanced technical equipment in every village. Perhaps their trucks and vehicles are sometimes antiquated. But they use their equipment to the limit and get the job done.

That evening, having toured their facilities and having seen these fine volunteers in action, I threw yet another first impression overboard, inspired by these brave and unselfish Portuguese men and women who were so keen on risking their lives for the sake of helping others that they did it for free.

Chapter 6
GREEN WINE AND
PURPLE GRAPES

I have often heard people say Portugal is a wine heaven. I can testify to the correctness of this statement in a Supreme Court without any fear of committing perjury.

In Portugal, I found out, two out of every hundred citizens own a winery of some sort and almost two out of every ten people work in a wine-related profession, be it wine, bottle or cork production!

Vineyards occupy nearly ten percent of the land. There are twelve demarcated regions and over fifteen non-demarcated regions in existence in Portugal. The excellent soil and humidity conditions of the country, together with the innumerable microclimates, provide the perfect conditions for the vine growing industry.

These figures are quite impressive, I have to admit. But what do they do with all this wine?

I remember sitting one afternoon in *Crossas,* a

restaurant in Areia -- a small village just east of the Guincho beach. The narrow dining room had three tables by the windows and four little booths squeezed in along the opposite wall. The wooden booths were separated by walls made of hollow, clay bricks. Bright green climbers decorated the wall edges.

Above the booths spanned a quasi-roof, quasi-shelf made of red wavy roof tiles. Lying along the valleys of the wavy tiles, as well as inside the hollows of the wall bricks, were many wine bottles of different regions. There must have been three to four hundred bottles there altogether. Between bites of the excellent veal steak I pondered why they had so many bottles there.

And then it all made sense. Around the far table, sat four businessmen, their suit jackets hanging nearby. They talked a lot and laughed quite often. Over their shoulders, I could see the tops of several wine bottles. I counted the bottlenecks. There were five of them! Five bottles divided by four diners equals… well, you get the picture.

Since then, I have been counting the bottles upon the tables wherever I went, and have found that for the Portuguese, finishing a bottle of wine per person during lunch is not an uncommon occurrence. After the meal they relax and chat for some time over coffee while the effects of the wine wear off.

A perfect example of this took place in Cascais. I was walking down the exceptionally lovely cobblestone narrow streets of the old town in search of a specific *tasca,* admiring the aesthetic ancient buildings, the colorful little doors and windows, as well as the breathtaking artistic tile decorations that appeared on the exterior walls here and there.

I nearly missed the small door that marked the inconspicuous entrance to the *tasca.* Inside, I found myself in a small room, perhaps twelve feet by twenty-five that once used to be a garage. There were six compact tables with several chairs neatly arranged around each. A large refrigerated glass display of wine bottles, soft drinks and desserts separated the dining area from the kitchen, which was a tiny room in the back. How did the owner fit a restaurant inside a garage was beyond me, but he managed it somehow and strangely it felt rather homelike.

Two businessmen sat in the far corner, engaged with their main course. A man in a green striped shirt occupied the table near mine, eating a salad. Two other fellows in short-sleeved shirts sat each by a table across the way and appeared to already be done with their lunch.

I ordered some white wine and it came in a porcelain pitcher with black lettering upon it announcing it was the wine of the house. The wine was excellent and gave the good meal a fancy quality. While I was eating, I watched the ongoing festival with amusement. Each table had either an empty bottle of wine or an empty pitcher on top, but the diners were far from drunk. They were merely high-spirited.

The men were talking cheerfully to each other

across the small room, as if they were all sitting around one large table. The owner/waiter joined in frequently and when one of the men started talking about his return trip from the Southern beaches over the weekend, the cook (the owner's wife) came out from the kitchen momentarily and added her own two cents to the conversation.

For a moment, I got confused, thinking that I wasn't in a restaurant but in somebody's home for a family lunch. The conversation changed gears as the businessmen finished their main course and were now free to talk. The ongoing discussion was always lively and pleasant.

The only time it became slightly tense was when I innocently asked the man in the green-striped shirt if he was a fan of the soccer club Sporting (whose color is green.) I didn't realize until it was too late that my question was nearly an insult; he was a fan of the Setúbal team. I recommend refraining from any soccer talk with Portuguese strangers.

But things simmered down rather rapidly and the friendly chat resumed once more. I realized as I finished my meal, that I ate faster than any of them. Even though everyone was in the middle of the meal or already done when I first walked in, they were still lingering over coffee when I left.

To my surprise, on my way out the smiling faces bid me farewell and wished me a happy afternoon. I returned the greeting and thanked them for their company. They were the living proof that a meal is much more enjoyable when one drinks wine along with it and chats over a *café* (or a *carioca de limão*) after it, in order to let the wine's influence mellow.

Now, the wine varieties in Portugal are so numerous that one never gets bored. There are many families who grow vines in their back yards and produce the wine right at home. The taste of the wine is different from one yard to the other.

Most restaurants in Portugal offer a *vinho da casa*, the wine of the house. It is sometimes served in a pitcher or in an unlabeled bottle, in which case the wine is from a small winery in the area. Or it will be a table wine in a labeled bottle, which the owner recommends, and in that case it will be cheaper than the other wines. Either way, each restaurant differs from the others with their wines of the house, and one is in for a little surprise whenever one dines in a new restaurant.

However, if you are not in search of surprises, it is quite acceptable in Portugal to describe to the waiter the kind of wine you like (and perhaps the price range) and he will usually recommend a good wine for your taste (and pocket.)

I have found that for some mysterious reason, half bottles in Portugal are expensive in comparison to the price of a full bottle.   "It would be such a waste to get half a bottle when for a few hundred more *escudos* I could get an entire bottle," say Portuguese and foreigner alike after looking over the wine list. It gives one a good reason to drink a full bottle.

With endless offers of wine at every corner, I

turned into a wine lover soon after my arrival in Portugal. Beer and liquor lost its appeal after the first glass of superb wine. Why waste my dear money on a few glasses of beer when for the same price I could get a bottle of good wine and really enjoy myself? Wine doesn't give one a bloated feeling, it has more class and if it is red wine and is older than five years it is even healthy!

Having been successfully converted, I decided to pursue my liking of this smooth liquid and research, for the sake of my readers of course, the different wines of Portugal. While surveying and trying scores of wines, two very interesting types emerged as Portuguese specialties, which I earnestly recommend.

Rather unfamiliar around the world, the first one is the *vinho verde*. Literally meaning "green wine," its name is somewhat of a misnomer. The wine color is not really green but is more transparent with light green hues; in fact, it is sometimes even red. *Vinho verde* is thus a name of the wine produced in a specific region and the "green" refers to its un-matured state (as opposed to ripe.)

The Vinhos Verdes district is an area stretching from Porto to the north as far as the Spanish border and from the coast to the east about fifty kilometers. The origin of this wine traces back to Roman times when evidence shows the special way of growing and harvesting of vines in that region was little known to the rest of the world at that time.

The uncommon vine-propping method called

"hanging" has been used for thousands of years to raise the vine runners above the ground. This system utilizes trees (such as oaks and chestnuts) for the support of the vine branches. The vine runners climb up the tree trunk and then hang from its branches as if they are part of it.

Green wine is low in alcohol content (8° to 11.5°) and high in fixed acidity, and consequently has a tart and sharp taste, as well as a bubbly characteristic. It does not resemble mature wine and is light, smooth and refreshing. It is most often chosen to accompany shellfish.

Vinho verde is drunk the most during the summer months and in unusually warm winter days. On a hot day with the sun baking your scalp, the thing to do is to open an extra-chilled bottle of green wine the temperature of which is such that condensation drops form around it. Then you will find this wine almost miraculous.

Once I was in Porto in August and even the evening was rather hot. Following my thirst, I found myself in a small bar in the old section of town by the river. Not only was it small, but it was also crowded. The people were engaged in lively conversations while the owner was busy preparing grilled pork steaks and filling up wine and beer glasses.

I managed to find a seat and ordered a bottle of green wine. The seats were actually short stools and the wooden tables were smallish. The arched ceilings of the bar, the narrow steps which led to the even smaller second floor, and the simple furniture made it seem like it was an old tavern from centuries ago.

The waiter returned with a wineglass, a large green unlabeled bottle and some napkins. I filled the glass with the greenish potion and noticed the slight bubbly activity upon pouring. It had a faint fruity aroma but had a wild taste. The cold liquid permeated my mouth, its acidic but pleasant flavor instantly turning my thirsty slouch into a refreshed, invigorated posture. The hardly noticeable bubbles were gentle and soothing.

Due to its low alcohol content, I was able to drink four glasses without much effect. I still enjoyed myself tremendously for the rest of the evening. *Vinho verde* is truly the best wine when "revival from the dehydrated" is in order.

So the next time you find yourself sitting in a café or a restaurant on a hot summer day, remember that when all other wines are forgotten and left in the cellars, *vinho verde* always offers an opportunity to quench your thirst in style.

The second fascinating wine is the *Moscatel de Setúbal*, the jewel in the Portuguese crown of wine making. Numerous tales of this heavenly wine had been whispered in my ear and I eventually decided to visit one of the long-established wineries that produced it.

Located in the center of Vila Fresca de Azeitão, a small town about ten kilometers west of Setúbal, the humble structure of the cellars was hard to find. Unlike the Port wine houses in Porto whose banners scream their label names across the River Douro, this elongated building had a single inconspicuous sign. *"Cave de J.M da Fonseca, visite-nos"* (J.M da Fonseca cellars, visit us) said the tastefully designed lettering across it.

The two-story old edifice was decorated the traditional way and had elaborate designs of tile and detailed paintings across its facade. With growing interest I passed through the double doors in the center of this unpretentious structure.

The lobby inside was dark and homey, where heavy wooden furniture around the spacious room provided sitting room for the guests. A small group of tourists were looking at the sizeable polished timber display shelves that presented various wine medals and awards. Moments later, our guide showed up and took us on a tour of the cellars.

The house was founded by José Maria da Fonseca in 1834. A graduate of the Coimbra University at the time, he was sent to Azeitão to take care of his father's agricultural properties. His interest in vines grew and soon he started his own winery there.

José Maria da Fonseca was one of the first in Europe to start shipping his wines abroad in bottles (it was mostly done in casks at that time) and his company became the first table wine company in Portugal. Currently it is owned and managed by his descendants.

The *Moscatel de Setúbal* is a special fortified wine produced only in Setúbal. It is often copied in the small wineries of the northern Alentejo, but can only be officially produced in the surroundings of Setúbal. It is high in alcohol content ranging from 12° to 17.5° and is also very sweet.

Moscatel is produced by a special process. The

wine is composed of several types of grapes which are blended with a minimun of 70% of *moscatel de Setúbal* grapes. The wine is then left inside a barrel in contact with the grape skins for a period of five months. Adding brandy at the appropriate moment, when the residual sugar and the alcohol contents reach the desirable levels, stops the fermentation. Thus the *moscatel* is both sweet and fruity.

Aging is then begun inside casks in the cellars. The cask sides are made of mahogany which gives the cask its strength while the lids are made of oak that lets the wine breathe during the aging process.

Rows upon rows of casks revealed themselves once I stepped into the dark, cool cellar. Each cask was marked in white chalk as to the year and type of its contents. Complex spiderwebs proved that the casks had not been moved since they were originally put there.

It was very important to keep the temperature inside the cellar at around 12°C. To accomplish this, the cellar is built of thick walls and located where it is away from any sources of heat. Lamps are used sparingly due to the heat they produce.

The wine "breathes" through the casks. Constant airflow is of extreme importance and any smells that linger in the air can penetrate through the wood and affect the wine's aroma. The cellars must, then, be additionally located far from any potential odor sources. Air vents at the top of the casks are covered in fine mesh to prevent the entrance of insects or dust particles.

A few minutes later the tour ended with a tasting

of some red and white wines. Once the other visitors left, I managed to get some additional information from the friendly tour guide.

"There are three types of *moscateis*," she said. "The Young Vintage, the Twenty-year Old Blend and the Superior Vintage."

The Young Vintage was a harvest of grapes from a single year that is older than four years. The Twenty-year Old is a blend of vintages, the youngest of which is at least twenty years old. The Superior Vintage is a harvest of one specific year and is older than twenty-five years.

But to appreciate these wines I had to taste them for myself, she said to my delight. It was therefore agreed that since it was lunchtime, I would come back around three o'clock for a tasting. This would also give her a chance to chill the wines so that I could taste them as they should be served.

Content with my newfound information, I left the cellars in search of lunch. Across the street I found a traditional little restaurant called "*O Alface*." It was a simple place with two small dining rooms, and in between them there was a bar where one could stand and drink a coffee.

I sat down at one of the sturdy tables and having studied the menu briefly, placed my order. The very friendly waiter (who was the restaurant's owner as well) nodded and went back to the kitchen. He returned moments later with a large smile and a large bowl with the soup of the day. It was *caldo verde*, a creamy potato and cabbage soup. Across the room, a picture of him and his wife in Holland hung on the wall. He cheerfully told me the story behind it while I was consuming the delicious soup in front of me. It was while they were visiting a family member there, he explained, that they got dressed in traditional Dutch clothing and had their picture taken.

I asked for a glass of Periquita wine with my meal, which was another special wine produced by J.M da Fonseca. It was a red wine and had a fresh berry aroma. Its taste was full and slightly sharp with a medium final palate. It is made from a particular type of grape originally found only in Azeitão, but which later on spread to other regions. I recommend it as a red wine.

My entrée, *lulas à Sevilhana,* arrived soon after. It was a huge dish of fried squids, french fries, rice and a side salad. I reflected again at my inability to predict the sizes of the meals despite the many times I have fallen for the trick. However, it was better to have too large of a dish than a small one, I concluded, and began eating.

The squids were terrific, their fried crispy covers contrasting with the soft white meat. They were obviously prepared by a chef as the taste was outstanding. The chef, I discovered later, was *Senhor* Alface's wife and she operated the entire kitchen by herself. God bless her, I thought as I was enjoying my meal.

So savory was the food that I actually finished my serving with some sense of accomplishment. Over a carioca de limão, Mr. Alface introduced me to the local specialty, a dessert called *torta de Azeitão*. It was a soft dough pastry in the shape of a hot dog, with a mixture of almond paste and eggs as a filling. It was quite good, even though I generally don't like desserts made with eggs.

Having thanked him for his personal service and having made a mental note of *"O Alface"* as a good restaurant, I made my way back to the Fonseca cellars in high hopes.

Inside I was directed to a building within the property where I found my kind tour guide standing behind a counter. A display of the complete array of wines produced by J.M da Fonseca was neatly arranged under the glass top of the wooden counter. Again, the room was dark and cool but its walls were tastefully decorated with items connected with winemaking.

The lady disappeared momentarily and returned with a silver tray carrying several wine bottles and glasses. I licked my lips in anticipation. I declined the offered spit bucket. I wanted to feel the wine's influence on my senses, not only on my tongue.

The first was the Young Vintage. It is usually served at 10°C as an aperitif or at 18°C as a dessert wine. This one was a 1991 *moscatel*. It had a clear topaz color and a fresh orange peel aroma. I sipped and let the chilled liquid roll in my mouth for a moment.

This wine was better than any other I have drunk in the past. The first taste was sweet and fruity. As I swallowed, it proved to be smooth and velvety. The final palate was heavier and very long.

After some time, came the twenty-year old *moscatel*. Slightly chilled, it was more of a dessert wine. I nearly got knocked out when I breathed in its aroma of fruits and nuts with a lot of alcohol.

Upon tasting, I could discern traces of fruity flavor followed by a mild burning-like sensation from the aged alcohol. The rich wine was very smooth when it rolled down my throat. A few seconds later I could feel a tingle run through my body as the wine made its way into the bloodstream.

Although the old and young had the same alcohol content, the older had more "impact," a quality achieved solely through aging. This *moscatel* wasn't fooling around, I thought. The final palate refused to disappear and was still going strong minutes later.

Slightly light-headed by now, I conversed with the lady for a bit about wines and other subjects that for some reason (the wine possibly?) elude my memory. The *moscatel*, she said, was one of the Portuguese's favorites, especially when it was served slightly chilled at the beginning of the meal. And I couldn't blame them. Its sweet and smooth nature made for an excellent refresher.

"So is *Moscatel de Setúbal* a white or a red wine?" I asked as soon as my head cleared up sufficiently.

"It is neither. It is just *moscatel*."

"But it is closer to white wine, isn't it?" I insisted.

"Well," she paused for a moment in thought.

"Actually, there is one type of *moscatel* which is

made of red grapes, but it is hardly known even to the wine connoisseurs."

My curiosity stirred. I asked her to explain further.

"*Moscatel Roxo* is its name. It stands for "purple moscatel" and is the official name of the grape variety as well. This grape is almost extinct, with a small vineyard of four hectares in Azeitão being the only one in existence in the world. It is a very special wine."

At that point, I was certain I was onto something good.

Served best as a dessert wine at a temperature of 20ºC, this special treasure was only sold as a twenty-year old wine. No younger *Moscatel Roxos* are produced. As if reading my mind, she asked if I wanted to taste it. I agreed resignedly, attempting not to appear too eager.

She disappeared again for a moment and returned with a half bottle and another glass. To my surprise, the color of the wine was amber with greenish tints and was only slightly darker than the twenty-year old regular *moscatel*.

"The grape is purple and so the wine is not as dark as red wine. However, when you taste it you will see how different it is from any other wine," she explained with a smile.

I held the glass close and breathed in the aroma. It was a strong exotic blend of scents, of which caramel, orange, fruit and sweet spices were the ones I could recognize. I sipped the delicate wine, and at once felt the soft and fruity palate. It was smooth and round as if the little drops had never become one but singly moved about in my mouth. The aftertaste was very long and lasted for nearly ten minutes.

This wine was indeed something else. With its unique color, its incredible aroma and the singular taste, it seemed to have noble characteristics, as if it was created with very important people in mind. I truly felt like a king with the glass of *Moscatel Roxo* in my hand and its palate still present in my mouth.

Although it was prepared using the same procedure as the regular moscatel, it had a slightly higher alcohol content (18°). It was also more sweet and fruity, and appeared to be more concentrated.

I purchased a bottle at once. Even the price was reasonable.

I thanked her sincerely for the interesting tour and for her friendly assistance. My research into the purple grape proved very fruitful, in both senses.

In my car, I laid the bottle gently in a secure position beside me as if it was a baby. I drove off, cheerful and satisfied with the results of my visit.

Wine is the only drink which the Bible mentions that was produced by Noah, Greek Mythology describes as created inside a volcano and the Lords of the Middle Ages designated as the symbol of luxury and well being.

But to this day I still wonder if the Bible, Greek Mythology and the Middle Ages Lords were referring to *Vinho Verde* or to *Moscatel de Setúbal*. In my opinion, it had to be one of the two.

Chapter 7
THE INDULGENCE RACE

The stopwatch was ready. The race was about to begin.

The challenge was immense. Would I be able to indulge myself in enjoying the essence of Portugal within a period of a mere twenty-four hours while remaining in Lisbon and its immediate vicinity? And "enjoy" meant enjoy with a capital E. No rushing, fussing, or cheating allowed. The time was nine o'clock in the morning. I was on my way.

My first destination was a little café in a section of Lisbon named Belém, the Portuguese word for Bethlehem. This small restaurant/coffee house was established in 1837 and has been the sole source for a mysterious confection called *pastéis de Belém*, using an old recipe developed centuries ago in the Convent of Jerónimos, located a block away from the café.

The secret formula for producing this special pastry was kept locked in a safe and known only by the owner and two loyal employees. Attempts to copy and make it elsewhere had been made without much success. Cafés across the country make and sell *pastéis de nata*, which is the basic form of the pastry, but by no means could that be compared to the original.

Many Portuguese who live abroad and come to visit Portugal make Café Pastéis de Belém their first stop in order to enjoy the much longed-for delicacy. Hundreds of Lisbon residents crowd this bustling coffee shop every morning of the year to relish the exquisite taste. Portuguese from North and South alike, flock in and buy large supplies of the *pastéis* to take back home with them.

Naturally, I had to experience the famous and outstanding wonder-pastry for myself. The café was located on *Rua de Belém*, faded blue awnings with small white lettering hanging over its four humble, undistinguished doorways. Already I could see the cue of people at the take-away section stretching outside.

I made my way through the busy entrance and sat at one of the few unoccupied tables in the dine-in area. After placing my order, two freshly baked *pastéis* and a drink, I went to peek at the take-away section, fascinated by how packed it was.

Looking over shoulders and in between heads, I managed to glimpse for a moment at the focus of attention. A large display stand presented the available pastries and sandwiches. Three waiters were rushing about behind it, taking orders, preparing the goods and packaging them in neat little white boxes.

An employee in blue overalls came by with a huge platter carried above his head and, squeezing by, laid the burden on a wide table behind the display counter. The platter carried close to two hundred fresh, out-of-the-oven *pastéis de Belém*. They were rapidly packed into white carton boxes, snatched away by the waiters as soon as packaged, and rapidly delivered to the hungering customers who were holding their breath in anticipation.

Within seconds the entire platter was empty and the man went back to the kitchen to fetch another one. Amazed, I returned eagerly to my seat. These little cakes must be out of this world and I couldn't wait to taste one of them. But my order hadn't arrived yet.

I surveyed the room around me. Good-sized wooden chairs and sturdy hardwood tables were used throughout the lively dining space, and each table was equipped with two cup-sized tin shakers. One was for sugar and the other for cinnamon, the traditional flavorings sprinkled over the *pastéis* for additional taste as desired.

The walls and ceilings were painted creamy orange, except for the main entrance's ceiling, which was of white plaster, embossed with different classic designs. The hallways between the three sections of the café were arch-shaped while the ceilings were either flat or vaulted.

A lovely layer of decorative tile covered the lower section of each wall up to about waist height. Various designs of flowers, animals and birds adorned the thin squares, all done with neat sky-blue coloring. Some of the tiles showed signs of wear and tear where the backs of chairs had been repeatedly pushed against the wall over the years. It seemed as if the place had been hardly modified since it first opened its doors, only the most vital repairs undertaken and the rest left untouched.

The waiter arrived with my order and briskly put everything on the table. The plate carried two warm *pastéis de Belém* atop a napkin. Each little cake looked like a small cup made of flaky dough, filled with a golden cream. Light-brown spots covered the top where it had been singed.

First I took a bite to taste the pastry without the extras. The crusty edges were fresh and delicate, the rich cream dissolved smoothly in my mouth. The taste was heavenly.   I then sprinkled some cinnamon and sugar on top. Another bite proved the taste remained just as divine, the interesting twist of cinnamon only adding to it.

It wasn't difficult to understand why Pastéis de Belém were so popular. I devoured the rest of my *pastéis* without delay and ordered a box of them for the way. I truly enjoyed this first item on my Best of Portugal list. I left, certain I would be back again as soon as possible.

It was almost ten o'clock, time for Lisbon's shop owners to be lazily crawling out of bed. By the time I arrived at the walking streets area known as the *Baixa*, the majority of the stores should be open, I reasoned.

I parked my car in the underground parking lot, and followed the stairs up to Lisbon's posh shopping center. Antique and impressive, this block of several interconnected walking streets had been restored to capture, in appearance at least, the spirit of centuries ago.

Large and small shops occupied the bottom floors of the ancient buildings, blending in with the surroundings rather than standing out with flashing fluorescent banners of modernity.

I strolled down the cobblestone walkways, looking over tastefully designed window displays, surveying menus framed in thin wood outside little restaurants and gazing at the piles of fresh pastries through the large glass panes of small *pastelarias* and cafés.

Walking in and out of stores wasn't a hassle. The owners and salesmen didn't leap on me or bother me with endless questions. I was allowed to look around without pressure and was treated cordially wherever I went. The merchandise, I found, was of good quality in most cases.

After several hours of quenching my eyes' thirst and, to my relief, avoiding an extravagant spending spree, I walked back to my car carrying a few supposedly much needed items I had eventually purchased.

My stomach, a travel companion of great influence, announced with determination it was time for lunch. As everybody knows, one can't argue with one's stomach, especially in Portugal. I followed the call to a restaurant in Restelo called the *Mercado do Peixe*, the fish market.

It was a fancy seafood specialty restaurant, one of the best in Lisbon, if not the best. As I entered, the maitre d' welcomed me with a large smile. The restaurant was spacious and empty. I was perplexed. The headwaiter explained at once that I was slightly early. It was merely half past twelve. By one-thirty the dining room should be packed, he promised.

I followed him toward the center of the restaurant. Well-constructed wooden furniture was used throughout. A dozen waiters were scurrying about, setting tables, straightening silverware, adjusting seats and placing 'Reserved' signs in the appropriate locations. It was much like entering a beehive, I reflected.

The maitre d' gestured toward a wide and longish table. I moved closer only to find a neat array of fish and mollusks on display. From the tiniest fish, heaped up in a separate tray for each type, to the huge ones who took up entire trays for themselves, they all seemed fresh and wholesome. Numerous trays presented various sorts of shellfish, from small shrimp to large live lobsters. A sizeable water tank nearby hosted an overplus of lobsters and crabs.

An immense grill stood boldly next to the water tank, visible and conspicuous for those diners who cared to examine how their meal was prepared.

The *Imperador,* the best fish they had that day, was suggested enthusiastically. It was a fleshy fish and traces of red mixed in with the bright white of its skin. I agreed and having chosen my main course was led to the table. I selected a white wine to go with the fish and off the maitre d' went.

With a view of the neighboring hills, slightly hidden by the nearby trees, I sat back in my chair and relaxed. A few minutes later a basket of bread, a bowl of grilled red and green peppers and a plate of cheese had arrived.

In the basket, the fresh half-loaves of thick white bread and yellow corn bread were still warm. The grilled peppers were outstanding; with the garlic and olive oil sauce, this superb concoction was beyond description. The dry cheese proved to be pungent but combined well with the bread and the peppers. I finished the appetizers in minutes.

The dining room was gradually filling up with businessmen, executives, and others who love excellent seafood. Here I must warn the reader that the price for this refined cuisine was not cheap. But then again, all good things are usually expensive.

I was quite full when the mammoth platter of entrée arrived, and I gaped at the sight of the serving's size. It was fit for at least two people, I was certain. How could I ever finish it?

One should beware of the sizes of portions in Portugal, especially in the Lisbon and Alentejo areas. They are never, ever skimpy. If they err, it is most definitely in the direction of larger quantities. It is a good idea while eating out in those regions, to discreetly peek at the main-dish sizes at the other tables before ordering (an option I did not have since there were no other diners around when I placed my order) or ask the waiter how large the portions are (an option I had forgotten to use). If very large, half a portion can be ordered in most restaurants. One portion could also be shared by two, or in extreme cases, by three people.

I attended to the *Imperador* at once, squeezing the lemon over the white meat. After the first bite, I forgot how full I had been only a few minutes before and a renewed feeling of hunger stirred within me. The meat was tender and grilled to perfection. It was neither dry nor soaked. The lemon and the superb sauce added an exotic taste. I was in seventh heaven.

Surprised at having eaten so much, I stared at the empty plate. It was then that I realized that I was totally immobile, the result of superb cuisine and wine consumption taken too far. I was about to ask for the wheel chair, when the waiter arrived, smiling, with the *sobremesa* (dessert) menu.

I declined gently (a mistake, no doubt) and instead ordered a *carioca de limão*. By now, the restaurant was packed and the score of waiters which had seemed excessive earlier, had to practically run from place to place to keep up with the hungry guests.

The *carioca de limão* finalized the meal rather well and I sat there for some time, staring into space, allowing the body to recover from the extravaganza. Without a doubt, it was a meal to remember for life.

The next destination was a region just south of Lisbon, perhaps an hour's drive away, give or take thirty minutes. The traffic in Lisbon, especially across the

Ponte 25 de Abril, is often heavily congested. I wouldn't recommend crossing the long structure more than twice a day if you value your sense of patience. Luckily, the odyssey along that suspension bridge took me only twenty minutes that afternoon.

My exact objective was to reach a certain cheese factory, *Quinta dos Vidais*, located on EN-10, about two kilometers west of Setúbal. I turned as soon as I saw the half-hidden entrance and pulled in at the gate. A low profile sign made out of tile confirmed that I had indeed arrived at the right *Quinta*.

I drove down the dirt road for about a hundred meters between vineyards and pastures where sheep were grazing peacefully, till I reached an arched gate leading to an inside courtyard. I parked and got out. At first it seemed completely deserted, a small dog yelping noisily was the only sign of life around.

However, a few minutes later, an older woman showed up at one of the doorways, a white apron tied around her waist and a white cap covering her silver-streaked hair. She welcomed me warmly with a smile and ushered me inside.

The room was full of various machines connected with cheese production as well as different utensils stacked upon wide shelves. An older man was adjusting one of the devices. He was introduced as *Senhor* Francisco Gomes while the lady presented herself as *Senhora* Feliciana Jerónimo.

I asked if they produced the famous cheese *Queijo de Azeitão* there. In Portugal, *Queijo de Azeitão* and *Queijo da Serra* are considered the best types of cheese. Azeitão cheese, being produced close by and therefore cheaper, was the perfect choice for a delicacy in the Lisbon area. Yes, she nodded affirmatively, they did make that fine cheese. In fact, they were the only *queijaria* (cheese factory) in the area which produced this cheese during the summer. Others did not usually operate in the months of June, July and August.

The *Senhora* was in the process of making the cheese in actual fact, and if I could wait a moment she would be right with me, she said. She was stooping over a large metal basin half full with milk, passing some sort of a sieve back and forth through the milk.

As I was interested in how it was produced, I asked her to show me what she was doing if it wasn't too much trouble. She readily agreed and explained to me what was going on. The fresh milk had arrived a few hours earlier and was heated up in a special machine for a while.

The local pastures had unique qualities which could not be found in other regions. Thus the sheep's milk from that area was the only one which could be used in making the Azeitão cheese, she added with a learned smile.

Having been transferred into the basin and mixed in with a special plant extract, the milk began to curdle. She explained that this extract was the ingredient responsible for the exceptional taste of the Azeitão cheese.

And now, she said, it was time to sieve the curds

out of the liquid. Using the utensil she was holding, the excess liquid was squeezed out, separating out the curdled milk. Then she packed the white chunks into plastic cylinders the size of beer mugs, and drained the basin through a finer sieve, making sure any little curds which slipped through earlier, were added into the plastic containers.

Out of a hundred liters of milk only sixty liters of cheese would be produced, so every gram was important, she pointed out solemnly. It must be, I reflected, as the price of one delicious kilo was about twenty dollars.

With the help of *Senhor* Gomes, the plastic cases were closed with their plastic lids and placed in a row, one after the other, on top of a railing that was connected to a machine. The machine squeezed the row of containers under a specified pressure for a certain length of time, thus compressing the cheese and ridding it of any excess whey still remaining.

Once the cheese was adequately squeezed, the containers were taken out of the machine and their lids taken off. The cheeses rolled out of their plastic cases, already shaped as short cylinders about four inches wide and two inches high.

The tiny cheese slabs were then neatly arranged on grill-like trays and carried into a large walk-in fridge where they would stay for ten days. Once out of the chilled room, they would be moved into an unrefrigerated room for a period of twelve days, after which they would get individually wrapped up and shipped off to the retailers. The goat cheese, which was the other kind they produced, went through the same process but was curdled with an enzyme rather than using a plant extract.

She cut me a piece of Azeitão cheese to taste. The outer layer was flexible but hard, while the inside was soft and creamy. I placed it in my mouth and it melted away like butter, the exceptional taste perceptible at once. The cheese was justifiably regarded as the best.

I thanked her profusely for the instructional tour and bought two Azeitão cheeses and one goat cheese.

"Would you like to taste my home-made *moscatel* wine?" *Senhor* Gomes' question took me by surprise. The question was comparable to asking a child if he wanted some candy.

" Most certainly," I responded without a thought.

He returned a few moments later with a wine bottle and a small glass, which he promptly filled and handed over.

I smelled the wine. The sweet aroma was inviting. I took a sip and let it roll in my mouth. It was deliciously sweet, the after-effect reaching my head belatedly. I congratulated him for this most excellent creation and expressed my utter satisfaction. He smiled and offered me the entire bottle, much to my disbelief. I accepted with pleasure.

Senhora Feliciana disappeared for a moment and returned with two cheeses. The first was a dried Azeitão cheese and the other a dried goat cheese. If one cut a piece off the cheese and left it out for a day or two, the cheese would dry up and acquire a completely different taste, she explained. I tried a piece of the dry Azeitão, and though similar in taste to the fresh one, it was sharper and more intense. The dry goat cheese was unlike the fresh one, but it was still quite good.

I placed my treasures inside a small cooler I had in my car and thanked them deeply for their wonderful hospitality, stressing how grateful I was for their time and assistance. Feeling cheerful and slightly light-headed, I hopped in my car and drove off, waving goodbye to both *Senhor* and *Senhora*.

So far, my mission had been progressing successfully.

Next, I headed to the Setubal market. Located in an elongated two-story building, this hub of bustle and lively commerce was filled with stands of all imaginable sorts. Fish, snails, shellfish, meat, vegetables and fruit were stacked above stands and tables. Clothes, sportswear and swimming suits hung in display in hallways where stands had been improvised. Several cafés were situated on the U-shaped second floor overlooking the market. At one of the bread shops, I bought a loaf of fresh Alentejo bread.

Fully equipped with bread, cheese and wine, I headed on to my next destination. Following the signs carefully and avoiding by sheer luck any brushes with the Little Man from the Signage Department, I arrived shortly after at the *Serra da Arrabida*, the Arrabida mountain range.

The mountains of Arrabida have unique vegetation. Wild shrubs and short trees grow closely together, creating a dense and thick overlay. In fact, *Serra da Arrabida* is a nature reserve, being the sole worldwide habitat for several types of plants.

Driving along 379-1, the road ascending rapidly to a height of five hundred meters, the magnificent view of the expanse of deep-blue sea gradually revealed itself. To the east, the peninsula of Troia with its golden sandy beaches, stretched far south, where it disappeared under a layer of clouds.

The long and narrow road twisted about, often ascending and descending, following the mountains' contours. Driving in Arrabida was never boring; I would vouch for that.

Narrow strips of dirt frequently appeared on the other side of the road, along the edges of the mountainside, offering many opportunities to park and admire the view. I carefully stopped at one of those spots, avoiding the edge beyond which the void below measured hundreds of meters.

I took in a deep breath, the pure air and the delicate scent of the singular vegetation filling my lungs. The contrast between the blanket of green vegetation and the intense blue vastness of the sea was simultaneously clashing and harmonious. Not a voice or sound could be heard, apart from the occasional bird chirp. So absolute was the silence that an oil tanker kilometers out in the ocean could be heard starting its engines.

Evening was approaching and I decided to bring out the goodies that would constitute my meal. The cheese and wine were brought out of the cooler, the bread taken out of its wrapping and the delicious dinner was served. Cutting a round notch through the top of the cheese's skin, I gained access to the creamy part inside while the harder shell served as a natural container. With the Alentejo bread, the chilled *moscatel* and the box of *pastéis de Belém* for dessert, I enjoyed myself with a capital E and an exclamation point, the pleasant sounds and views of nature complementing the perfect ingredients to make a perfect meal.

An hour later, the twilight was casting hues of orange and red across the horizon while I was meticulously packing away the remains of my meal. My Fiat's engine was soon purring and I was on my way back to Lisbon.

I carried on along 379-1, enjoying the fabulous panoramic vistas of Arrabida the entire way, then followed EN-10 onto the highway. It was already dark when I crossed the *Ponte 25 Abril* and the breathtaking sight of Lisbon bathing in lights stretched below me. That in itself was well worth the trip.

I had agreed to meet with my friend, Thomas, in a local café around ten p.m. and I was a bit early. I drank a *carioca de limão* while waiting and looked back on what I had achieved so far with satisfaction. I could have easily called it a day, but not in Lisbon. The day in Lisbon begins with nightfall.

Thomas showed up a bit late but that didn't worry me at all. As I was already immune to the Portuguese tardiness I mentioned nothing of time and greeted him cheerfully instead. He sat down and ordered a drink as well. Many of his friends came, exchanged a few words and went their way. Eventually two of them joined us and when the café closed, we all went to Thomas' house. There we lingered for some time, played soccer with the dog in the back yard and listened to reggae music. Around one o'clock we set off into the night.

First we dropped by Docas. Located by a marina along *Avenida 24 de Julho*, directly below the *Ponte 25 de Abril*, Docas is a collection of cafés, restaurants and disco bars, situated one next to the other along the spacious marina main quay.

It was aesthetically designed, the cafés and restaurants located on one side of the dock, farther from the water. Across the way and on an elevated wooden platform, the numerous table and chair set-ups of each coffee shop and restaurant occupied the side of the wharf closer to the water, overlooking the marina. In between, the quay itself provided a wide path for the flocks of visitors.

We sat at one of the tables outside and ordered a few drinks. We stayed there for over an hour, drinking, talking, and looking at the people walking about. The sounds of a hundred conversations, the distant noises of cars and motorcycles, as well as the mixture of the different tunes and melodies emanating from the disco bars filled the air around us.

It was three o'clock and the night was still very young.

From there we went to a disco club named Kapital, just across the road from Docas. We danced and had a good time for several hours, the crowded club surprisingly full of older and younger people alike.

When we came out, it was six o'clock and traces of dawn could be seen across the eastern skies. I was sure my chapter was coming to a close, but my assumption was completely unfounded. The Portuguese took partying very seriously. Dawn was a bit too early to quit.

We made our way to yet another disco club and there had even more fun with two nice ladies we met (sorry, the editor censored the details). Around eight o'clock we all celebrated the end of the night by having breakfast in a nearby café, among people who had just woken up and were drinking the first coffee of the day on their way to work.

By nine o'clock I arrived at home, my mission accomplished. Tired but satisfied, I slumped onto bed in total and helpless exhaustion. My last thought before closing my eyes was that in the future, I should rest a few days prior to undertaking such a task as a twenty-four hour indulgence race around Lisbon.

Chapter 8
THE ART OF STOPPING A RAGING BULL

Despite my firm anti-bullfight policy, I was persuaded to go and watch a Portuguese bullfight, which is quite different than the Spanish one.

"In Portugal," a friend told me, "not only do the bullfighters not kill the bull but they have to personally stop the charging 'locomotive' without any weapons or means of defense."

"Yeah, and cows live on the moon," I said sarcastically. No one in their right mind would ever attempt to bring a half-ton bull to a halt with his bare hands. I can tell when someone is trying to pull my leg.

Disregarding my rebuttal, he went on to add that in Portugal, slaying the beast in the ring meant time in jail. Assured the bull would not be killed right in front of my eyes, I agreed to go. And so I found myself on a lovely Saturday afternoon waiting outside the bullring, not quite knowing what to expect.

The event started way ahead of the actual fight.

Hundreds of people were gathered about the sidewalk with their tickets in hand, waiting for the main doors to open. The men chatted away with each other about the quality of the participating bulls, argued whether the bullfighters' recent performances promised an interesting show that day or not, and generally discussed the horses' lineage and descent. The women didn't talk about cooking or sewing but instead had their own arguments about the forecasted quality of the bullfight.

A friendly man stood behind his food stand, offering small paper bags of peanuts, sunflower seeds and fried broad beans. His stand had also the familiar white paper-wrapped packets of the *Queijadas de Sintra*, as well as soft drinks.

Having purchased some peanuts and a drink, I read over the program that an older man was distributing around. It announced the bulls' names, their age, weight and which farm they came from, with a picture of each. The names and portrait photos of each bullfighter appeared at the bottom of the leaflet.

An old man was walking about, selling hats and seats. The headwear type was the popular *boné*, a soft round beret with a short brim protruding over the forehead. The seats were not really seats but small plump cushions.

"After a few hours of perching on a concrete slab, one's behind rebels against the cruelty, unless provided with a pillow," said the old man sagely.

I thanked him for his kind warning and informed him my rear was willing to suffer quietly, but bought one of his hats as the sun was quite hot that day. How could they have the tiers made of concrete alone? Surely there was at least some padding, even if only plastic, I assured myself.

I finished an entire sack of peanuts before the gates were finally pulled open and I quickly got to my assigned "seat", which indeed proved to be a number scribbled on the bare cement row. I gaped with disbelief. Where was that old man again, I quickly looked around in vain. He was nowhere to be found and I was doomed.

Nevertheless, my spirits remained unspoiled. People were briskly finding their places and sitting down, some without cushions (phew, I wasn't the only one.) Kids were running around, arming themselves with ice creams and *Queijadas* they purchased from the nomadic vendors which endlessly circled the stadium with their merchandise. The men were still in the heat of the argument about the quality of the bulls and the horses. Overall it was a lively and cheerful affair.

The rows descended in circles down to the first row where a high wall dropped ten feet down to the ring. A strong, shoulder-high and circular wooden fence, about six feet away from the wall, provided a protected corridor around the ring. Numerous people wearing different colored overalls, were keeping busy, cleaning or just moving about aimlessly, waiting for the fight to commence

The event was dedicated to the local fire department whose band was present. It started playing a few folk tunes to signal the event was about to start. The last few spectators took their seats and after some time, three solemn men appeared in a special stand close by me.

They were the director of the bullfight, his assistant and the trumpeter. The latter would relay the commands of the director to the men inside the ring, using special trumpet signals. After getting situated and set up in their places, the director bid the fight to begin.

The sound of the trumpet signals resulted in the opening of the gates and in marched the dramatis personae, dressed in their respective brightly colored and traditional outfits, to the sound of vigorous clapping and optimistic hurrahs.

First entered several men carrying long poles with silk flags of various coats of arms, then came the *capa*s (the bullfighter's assistants with the capes) followed by the *cavaleiro*s (the horse-mounted bullfighters.) They all took off their hats and caps and presented themselves to the audience who cheered even louder. This form of bullfighting – on horseback – is typically Portuguese and not done in any other type of fights.

I stared with astonishment as the *cavaleiro*s rode around the ring, presenting their horses and showing off their paces. The horses were stepping sideways! Unbelievable as it was, those specially trained horses could walk sideways without stumbling, their long and slender legs crossing each other in a perfect and graceful fashion. Not only that but, to my growing surprise, they were even following the beat of the band.

The *cavaleiros* wore majestic gold-trimmed 18th century aristocratic outfits, long white wigs and wide triangular velvet hats decorating their heads. The *capas* were clothed in similarly ornamented costumes and walked with a noble stride. The horses were covered with glittering trappings. I concluded it was well worth coming if only to watch this glamorous ceremony.

The traditional stirrups of the *cavaleiros* were box-like and made of wood with one end open, and were the same ones that are used by the herders of the fighting bulls. The shoe-like stirrup provided the herders with comfort since they spent their entire day in the saddle. Additionally it protected their feet against the horns.

The smiling *cavaleiros* waved and disappeared through the gate. The *capas* and the rest of the crew soon followed, leaving the flat, earth-covered arena deserted again. The director gave a signal and the trumpeter relayed the message with a short toot.

The gate opened and out came four *capas*, this time leading a mule that carried two large wooden boxes. Once in the center of the ring, the boxes were unstrapped, carried over to the far side of the ring and laid behind the fence. While three *capas* led the mule off, the last one removed the box lids and brought out a *bandarilha*, a multi-colored, decorated spear, about four feet long.

He entered the ring again, *bandarilha* in one hand, cape in the other. He waited in the ring till the signal was given for the *cavaleiro* to enter. Having shed his heavy, flamboyant jacket and wearing a lighter, more comfortable one instead, the *cavaleiro* rode toward the *capa* and accepted the *bandarilha*. He approached a section of the stands and dedicated the fight to a distinguished and beautiful lady.

Another *capa* joined in and the trumpet sounded again. A wave of excitement swept through the stands, followed by a moment of silence. And then, resembling a launched missile, the bull charged furiously into the ring to the renewed cheering of the crowds.

It was huge, its black and massive body stout and powerful. The legs were short but lean; the neck was wide and muscular. The points of the two massive horns were sheathed in leather, rendering them less harmful. The half-ton bull was on the loose in the ring.

The first *capa* waved his cape at the bull, attracting its attention away from the *cavaleiro*. My heart skipped a few beats as the bull charged and the *capa* stepped out of the way at the last moment. The bull jabbed its head at the cape only to find nothing behind it.

Frustrated, the bull charged toward the other *capa*, who was calling it while flapping the cape. Again, the cape was the only thing the animal had managed to horn. The first *capa* was now the one to attract the bull's attention again and the unnerving routine repeated.

All the while, the *cavaleiro* stayed out of the bull's way, studying its behavior and performance. When he was content he had learned enough, he signaled to the *capa*s to cease their activity. They leaped over the fence with their capes, leaving the bull baffled at their disappearance. The beast cautiously approached the wooden wall to investigate where they had darted off.

Having located them and yet being unable to reach them, the bull repeatedly rammed at the fence with such force that I was sure the wooden structure would soon collapse, leaving the defenseless people behind it at the mercy of God. But it miraculously sustained the attacks.

The *cavaleiro* shouted and galloped in front of the bull in order to provoke the animal. The bull fixed his gaze upon his new enemy. It was larger and therefore easier to strike, reflected the beast slyly, and it didn't hold up a flapping cloth behind which it could so mysteriously vanish. Confident again, the bull stormed at the horse with fury.

The *cavaleiro* and the horse merely whisked away in a gallop, escaping the bull in the nick of time, luring it to follow them in their encircling motion. The bull, being slower and heavier, was not able to keep up with the horse's evasive maneuvers and slowed down to a halt, close to the fence.

The *cavaleiro* repeated this technique several times, attempting to make the bull run as much as possible with the purpose of tiring it and at the same time studying further its pattern of attack. And then the time came when the beast stopped at the center of the ring, its tongue hanging out.

The *cavaleiro* turned the horse around so it was facing the bull directly. Then came a series of hollers and chivvies intended to rouse the beast from its lethargy. Only when the bull was in motion, could the *cavaleiro* attack. The *cavaleiro* let out strange sounds of loud ridiculing laughter, until the locomotive at last began to charge.

I observed the scene with alarm, as both animals charged at each other. The *cavaleiro* urged the horse forward till the very last moment when he guided the horse to the left and out of the way.

The bull, realizing too late that his target was veering to the side, struggled in vain to change the inevitable course determined by the inertial force of five hundred kilos in full speed. Unable to follow the horse's quick moves, it missed it by inches, thrusting its head up in an unsuccessful attempt to score a partial hit, to the cheers of the audience and the sounds of the band. I took a deep breath in relief.

The *capa*s jumped over the fence and into the arena at once and diverted the bull's attention while the unscathed *cavaleiro* galloped around the ring in acknowledgement, holding up the *bandarilha*.

To my amazement, the bull was charging at the *capa* with more anger and force than before. The beast was furious beyond belief. I noticed the reason for its fury a moment later. A stub of the *bandarilha* was hooked under the animal's skin above the shoulder blades, spots of blood appearing around it. In the midst of all this turmoil, the *cavaleiro*'s arm had stretched out and lodged the *bandarilha* into the bull's shoulder muscle so quickly that I missed it entirely.

The *bandarilha* was designed to break close to the tip so that the shorter end hitched onto the bull while the longer piece remained in the *cavaleiro*'s grip. Having traded the broken used *bandarilha* for a new one, the *cavaleiro* began the ritual again by luring the bull into chasing him around the ring.

As soon as the beast stopped close to the center, the *cavaleiro* once more took his position facing the bull, *bandarilha* ready in hand. This time, the hit-and-run attack was even more daring. (I will attempt to describe it in slow motion.)

While charging at each other, perhaps twenty feet apart, the *cavaleiro* steered his horse to the right giving the bull enough time to adjust its course, only a second later to cause the horse to forcefully leap in the other direction, the bull only a few feet away. The horse sprang agilely to the left out of the way while the *cavaleiro* thrust the *bandarilha* home, the bull unaware yet of the rapid change, still charging onwards at full speed.

The thunder of applause for this risky display of courage and competence was gratefully accepted by the *cavaleiro*, who circled the ring once more (the equivalent of taking a bow,) while the *capa*s were distracting the enraged bull.

Another long *bandarilha* was successfully wedged into the animal using the same procedure, before the *cavaleiro* began with the short *bandarilhas*. These measured only half the length and didn't break off close to the tip. The *cavaleiro* had to lean down even more in order to hit the target.

However, prior to taking the *bandarilha*, this famous *cavaleiro* tied the horse's reins to his belt, and guided the horse over to the fence using his knees alone.

There he took two of the short *bandarilhas*, one in each hand, much to the shrieks of the anxious audience who anticipated what was to come.

I watched goggle-eyed as the *cavaleiro* positioned his horse without using the reins at all, so it was facing the bull on the opposite side of the ring. I covered my eyes (but peeked) as both beasts began their charge. At the last moment the horse leaped to the right while the *cavaleiro* shot the two short *bandarilhas* into the back of the bull's neck.

The majority of the audience, me included, rose to its feet as the *cavaleiro* and his horse emerged from the scene unharmed. The bull, enraged with his inability to strike the swift enemy, was energetically chasing the *capa*s. It was moving with a little less speed and control of its massive body, but the livid passion and burning rage inside the animal were only growing.

What a magnificent display of ability, I reflected. To command a horse by the use of one's knees and feet alone, while a raging bull is charging at one in full speed, is quite an achievement. At this point, the trumpet sounded and the proud *cavaleiro* with his superb horse left the ring to the sounds of the cheering audience.

A group of *forcado*s, eight guys in red vests, brown pants and white knee-high socks, jumped over the fence into the ring. With their green caps on, somewhat resembling the elves of Santa Claus, these brave fellows had a slightly tougher task than satisfying the younger population of the world on Christmas Eve.

One of them removed his cap and stepped closer

to the stands where he dedicated the fight to his father who was sitting at the front row. The *capas* had the bull on the opposite side of the ring and, seeing that the *forcados* were ready, leaped over the fence to safety. In the ring the eight men faced the beast with their bare hands. This part of the bullfight originated in and is unique to Portugal.

I gripped my knees with worry as the *forcados* formed a straight column, one directly behind each other, the first in line facing the bull across the ring. The animal was eyeing them with curiosity, puzzled at this new and unfamiliar target. They seemed much smaller, softer and vulnerable reasoned the bull with growing interest. Finally, something to sink the horns into with ease. They had only two legs and carried nothing except their little hats. Should be an easy catch, the animal concluded, gazing at them with keen alertness.

The first in line was of medium frame, neither thin nor fat, and weighed in my estimation perhaps eighty kilos. What was a mere eighty kilos compared to the massive five hundred, I pondered.

He seemed somewhat nervous at his fearsome task but yet was determined to execute it with honor. Having soberly fit the green cap on his head, the leader mentally prepared himself.

Then, resting his hands on his hips, the leader took a bold step toward the bull. The bull was watching attentively but didn't move one bit.

"*Olha touro!*" challenged the first in line, taking another step forward. But the bull remained immobile.

He took another two steps ahead, the second in line following but keeping a distance behind.

"*É touro!*" repeated the leader, by now halfway across the ring. The bull bellowed and kicked up dust with his right front foot in irritation, its tail whipping about.

The first in line shouted on, this time advancing several feet ahead, stamping his feet noisily in order to urge the bull into action.

The beast was violently thrusting its head about, goring the air around him, while remaining in the same exact position, exhibiting the violent and deadly horning it was capable of. I didn't envy the poor fellow facing the bull.

Another series of stamping caused a stir within the bull and without a warning, it burst into full-fledged attack. The *forcados'* leader took a few steps back so that he would be moving in the same direction as the bull, thus minimizing the impact.

At the last second, the leader jumped slightly in the air as the high-powered bull slammed into him. The man's arms locked rapidly around the bull's horns while his knees secured tightly around the beast's snout. The bull was violently jerking its head up in an attempt to shake off the man, who was holding on for dear life. The second in line jumped on the bull's head as well, hoping to slow down the locomotive.

Alas, so forceful was the bull's attack that it managed to toss the two men off to the ground and I gasped in horror as I watched it trying to gore them, luckily without success. The group dispersed at once in all directions. Some ran over to help the two on the ground.

The leader and the second in line, shaken and covered with the bull's blood, got to their feet quickly and regrouped with the others on the other side of the ring. They all rapidly took their positions, forming a line once again, as the leader squared away his stained cap on top of his head.

"*É touro!*" he boldly commenced the routine once more, not as nervous but surely more determined. The beast proved to be a tough nut to crack and a challenge. But he was going to bring that bull to a halt if it was the last thing he did.

I was biting my fingernails nervously as the courageous leader stepped closer of the bull, shouting at it as he went.

The bull charged again at full force. The *forcados'* leader repeated his trick and was holding onto the animal's head in an instant. The second in line was closer this time and at once jumped on as well. The rest of the group rushed forward and surrounding the bull's head, pushed forward with all their might, while one of them grabbed the bull's tail.

Regardless of their efforts, the bull wouldn't be stopped easily and it shoved them back for some distance, the tail man dragging behind as if water-skiing. The men were nearly slammed against the wooden barricade before they managed to slow the raging animal down and bring it to a complete halt.

Holding it down with a collective effort, they stood there for a minute until the bull stopped twisting its head about, accepting its defeat. The crowds were cheering with great respect and enthusiasm while the band played a merry tune.

Then with proper timing, they released the bull as one and took a safe distance from its harmful horns' range, the tail man still holding on. Without the restraint, the beast commenced charging in their direction, dragging the man behind him. But the weight on its tail was irritating. So it decided to focus on the pest behind, who was holding on with enduring persistence.

Swinging around like a dog chasing its tail, the bull attempted to reach him in vain. Once the others cleared the ring, the tail holder let go unexpectedly and proudly walked away, the bull standing there, baffled at what was occurring. Its enemy left the battlefield and leaped over the fence to safety.

A trumpet sound prompted the gates to open. The bull turned around rapidly to inquire as to the source of the clatter. In trotted five large cows, the bells that dangled around their necks producing sounds of grazing fields and meadows. Two men on horseback, dressed in herdsmen attire and carrying long herder poles, followed behind.

Driving the cows toward the bull, they tried to get it to join the herd. The bull, confused, seemed to gain interest in the cows around him. The men drove the cows toward the gate, but the bull wouldn't follow. It was still in the mood for war and nearly attacked one of the horsemen who managed to hide behind the cows.

After some minutes of driving the herd about and urging the bull to take up membership in it, they eventually persuaded the bull to follow the cows toward the gates. Even at the last moment, it lingered behind as the cows were leaving the ring, hesitating to follow and reluctant to exit. But it did eventually follow, the audience clapping fervently in appreciation of the good fight it had put up. The gates were at once shut behind it, leaving the ring empty and deserted.

Shortly after, the gates opened, ushering in the *cavaleiro*, the *capa*s and the leader of the *forcado*s to the sound of congratulatory music and applause. They started at the left side and walked around the entire ring slowly, waving their hats to the joyous crowds at each section, ensuring no one was missed.

As they went by, those who felt the performers had excelled tossed caps, *boné*s and even sweaters at their feet. The *cavaleiro*, the *forcados'* leader and the *capa*s were beaming with satisfaction as they threw the tokens of appreciation back to their owners. They completed their round and, filled with pride, knowing they had performed well and brought honor to their families' name, left the ring to the sound of the band playing cheerfully.

Feeling awe and respect for these brave bullfighters and at the same time pity and sorrow for the bull's pain, I sat there for some time with mixed emotions boiling inside of me.

Recalling a story I once read about the

Portuguese king Dom João II, who ruled toward the end of the fifteenth century, I found refuge in history. The story goes that the King and Queen were strolling one day in Alcochete towards the public square where a bullfight was to take place later on that day.   As they walked about casually, their courtiers and servants following in their footsteps, a raging bull escaped and was charging down the street, scattering a hysterical mob before it.

Those ahead of the procession disappeared with the crowd while those in the rear were lagging behind, engrossed in each other's company, unaware of what was occurring. The King and Queen remained facing the empty street and the approaching bull.

Dom João placed himself in front of the Queen and looked around for the page bearing his sword. The startled boy came forward with a jump, but his royal master, before taking the weapon, found time to tweak the young man's locks to teach him not to be absent-minded.

With sword in hand and cloak upon his arm, the King prepared to defend his wife. As it happened, though, the mad bull passed by without attempting to attack the group, and the members of the entourage emerged shame-facedly out of their hiding.

Bullfighting was a sport, and an art, born out of tradition and cattle herding, I finally concluded. And in that respect, it was a reminder that whether in a bull ring or in defense of one's wife, those with the courage and boldness to stand up to a dangerous threat regardless of the risk, would always be admired and revered with awe.

Chapter 9
SAINTS, SARDINES AND GARLIC THINGS

Portugal is full of Saints.

For example, *Santo António* (Saint Anthony) is the patron of Lisbon and some of its surrounding towns. His day is celebrated on the thirteenth of June. The twenty-fourth of June marks the day of *São João* (Saint John), the patron Saint of Porto and its suburbs. *São Pedro* (Saint Peter), the patron of Sintra, celebrates his day on the twenty-ninth of June. Many smaller towns and villages have their own Saints and their days are celebrated on the appropriate dates.

And if one thinks that these days are celebrated with solemn prayers alone, one is in for a surprise. These days are rather festive and joyous.

It was for this reason that on the eve of *Santo António* I headed toward the center of celebration, to closely inspect the ways of the Portuguese when it came to merrymaking.

Following the freeway in the direction of Lisbon's seven hills, I could already discern the diffused halo above the city, created by a thousand streetlamps, neon signs and house lights. From a distance it looked like a giant football stadium. As I was approaching the suburbs, I could already feel the spirit of celebration in the air.

The sidewalks were full of cheerful people. Colorful decorations spanned the streets, stretching from one lamppost across to another. Ornamented food stands with *Boas Festas* banners hanging above them, offered many ways to satiate one's hunger and thirst.

I followed the streets toward Alfama. Covering one of the seven hills, this ancient cluster of decrepit houses is the oldest district of Lisbon and had been the favorite spot for the aristocratic Moorish families during the eleventh century. A century later, Dom Afonso Henriques, Portugal's first king, drove the Moors out of Lisbon, and the summer palaces were replaced by churches, convents and hospitals.

Searching for a parking place was an adventure in itself. Many people parked outside Alfama and then walked the rest of the way but I was lucky and found a spot close by.

The houses along the narrow streets were of diverse design and color. The winding roads seemed to be chasing their tails, while arched bridges beneath allowed other streets to pass under them, forming a sort of multi-layered labyrinth.

It was easy to get the impression one had traveled back in time. Clothes and sheets were hanging from nylon lines outside the windows, cobblestoned roads dominated the district and tiny bustling shops were tucked neatly inside nooks, cramped between house entrances. Lampposts were about the only item which reminded one of this century. Walking along the alleys and the old flights of stairs which constituted some of the narrow streets was enchanting.

Traditional Portuguese music sounded from windows, balconies and restaurants, its gay and joyful lyrics encouraging the numerous merrymakers in their rejoicing. Tables were being set on the streets, open grills were being warmed up and wine bottles were being opened.

I found my way through the busy streets until I found what I was looking for: an improvised restaurant that was operating right outside a *pensão*. A row of four plastic tables and several chairs around each occupied a stretch of asphalt in front of the building. An old man, the owner, was attending to the grill at the end of the row while his elderly wife greeted me with a warm smile and placed a fresh tablecloth over my table. His two granddaughters were rushing about and assisting in serving the guests.

And this is where our little friend, the Sardine, came into the picture.

A large part of the *Santo António* celebration is of course the sardine festival. The sardine season usually starts in June and ends in August and that is the best time of the year to eat them. June, being the first month of the season, is when this poor fish suffers the biggest blow to its population. Fishermen all over Portugal cast their nets several times a day in the hope of catching as many sardines as possible. I wouldn't be surprised if the number of sardines in the Atlantic was cut in half during this much-dreaded month. If sardines had a calendar, I am sure the month of June would be omitted much like the thirteenth floor is sometimes omitted in skyscrapers.

I had been told a grilled sardine in Portugal was an experience not to be missed.

I ordered four sardines and started nibbling at the bread that had magically appeared on my table. I soon realized that I was in fact sitting and eating in the middle of the road. It was a strange feeling. Cars passed by once in a while, slowly driving along the narrow path that the many outside tables and parked automobiles had formed.

While waiting for my order, I decided to walk over to the grill and watch what the owner was doing. The grill consisted of a metal barrel cut in half that stood over four shaky wooden legs. The half-barrel was nearly full with hot black coals that glittered red and yellow here and there. On top lay two metal grids. These were joined together at one end and had long handles on the other, ten slightly crisped sardines lay in between.

The elder turned the grids over every few minutes and was talking to a friend who was even older. They had an open bottle of wine nearby and were taking turns drinking the red liquid. When the fish were ready I watched with amusement as these two fellows separated the two grids and unloaded the cooked sardines onto a silver platter. They each quickly devoured two sardines while the owner's wife wasn't watching and washed it down with some more wine.

I have never seen someone eat a fish so fast. It reminded me of the cat in the cartoons which opens up his mouth wide, slides an entire fish inside and partly closing his mouth, pulls out the skeleton by the tail.

The friend then walked over and presented the wife with the remaining six, which were immediately served at one of the tables. These fellows, I noticed with a smile, were having lots of fun while cooking. A drink here and a sardine there turn any task into an enjoyable one. Another dozen fresh sardines were placed carefully in between the grids.

"How long do you grill them for?" I asked the owner.

"Ah!" he started with a learned sigh. "There is an art to grilling sardines."

He drew closer as if someone was spying on us. With a knowing smile, he quickly turned over the new batch of fish.

"This is too early," he whispered, pointing at their scales. "They have to look sunburned, as if they have just returned from a long day at the beach."

I watched intently as he carried on.

"You must also pay attention that they don't stick to the grill," he said and lifting the top grid, moved each fish over slightly. There was a long pause due to another long sip of the wine.

"There, these are ready," he again pointed at the scales. They seemed reddish-brown but not charred. He winked and went ahead to eat one of them so as to prove his point. His friend showed up with the platter and the ritual repeated itself. This time four of the remaining sardines were mine.

I thanked the owner for the interesting lesson and went off to my table to try the taste for myself. Although one would readily agree an art of cooking sardines did exist and was vitally important, one couldn't negate the fact that eating them required more skill and expertise.

(If you are already an experienced sardine eater, you are free to skip the next few highly technical paragraphs.)

Place your sardine on a large enough piece of bread in the center of your plate. I recommend eating the first sardine without the nearly charred scales. Carefully peel the "skin" off, starting about the middle of the fish and work your way to the tail. The white flesh will reveal itself with a sort of a groove running along the center of the fish, under which the spine is hidden.

Slowly push the meat above the groove up. The meat will come off, leaving the majority of the bones behind. As a word of caution, the sardines have many small and flexible bones. Most of them turn into pulp in the chewing process. However, in the unlikely event a small bone does stay in your throat, either eat a small piece of potato or bread or flush it down with water. Usually this takes care of it.

I ate a small piece and the tender flesh tasted

surprisingly simple in my mouth. Its down-to-earth savor was rather remarkable. It wasn't rich or unique, neither complex nor sophisticated. It was just a good fish grilled to perfection. And I loved it. The old man knew what he was doing, I reflected.

I separated the rest of the flesh off the spine, from the middle to the tail. Unless one is an expert, which I wasn't, one is better off avoiding the part from the abdomen forward. Once done with one side, I turned it over and repeated the process with the untouched side. I tried pouring olive oil over the meat as was suggested to me by the older lady, and the taste was even better.

At times, the females have two batches of eggs in them that are somewhat salty and, depending on one's taste, delicious.

I finished my serving of sardines and ate the slice of bread that was sardine-flavored and damp with olive oil, and poured myself a glass of red wine. I relaxed back in my folding seat and watched the celebrants who were walking by, enjoying the music and the atmosphere.

A bit later, I made it to my feet and walked around the district. Wherever there was a vacant spot, stands of all sorts were erected. Next to the grand church of *São Miguel*, long tables were set up where large and small families sat and enjoyed the *sardinhada*, the sardine banquet.

Further ahead, there was a group of small merchant booths with all sorts of items on display, from fine leather goods to *manjericos*, tiny fresh basil plants that are usually given as presents on *Santo António* day due to their pleasant mint fragrance.

I bought a traditional deep fried pastry named *farturas*. It was a long, cigar-like confection that was made of dough, cinnamon and sugar. If one wished, it could be sprinkled with more sugar. I ate it without the additional flavoring and it was quite tasty, somewhat resembling a fried doughnut. Not the most nutritious dessert, I thought to myself, but once in a while it was all right. I strolled around for a while longer and managed to locate my car in the process.

During the evening I had seen hundreds of people. They were enjoying the food, the music and just mingling with the crowds. I noticed on frequent occasions how when one group of people met a group of friends they began their greetings with *beijinhos*, blocking the path for those behind them. A *beijinho* is the kiss on the cheek that replaces hand shaking. Sometimes it is two kisses, one on each cheek. Normally, men don't exchange *beijinhos*, unless closely related. But it seemed at times that everybody knew everyone else, and it was just one big family.

I left this cheerful and lively family around midnight, certain that in the south of Portugal, they knew how to celebrate and enjoy life.

How could I celebrate *Santo António* and then not join Porto in its *São João* festivities? I was asked.

Indeed, how could I? I asked myself.

I had kept in contact with my friend João from Porto whom I had met on Monte Gordo's beach in the first chapter, and it seemed like a good opportunity to call him up.

"Come on over, I will show you what is a real celebration!" he urged me over the phone. And so my friend Teresa and I were on our way the morning of the twenty-third, heading north on the *auto-estrada* A1 – the Lisbon-Porto highway.

The magnificent countryside landscape along the highway made the trip easy and pleasant. The road was comfortable and there were many opportunities to stop and drink a *carioca de limão* while my little Fiat caught its breath.

The three-hundred kilometer journey passed rather quickly and we arrived at Porto around one in the afternoon. We met João at the train station and both he and I were very happy to see each other again.

"The celebrations won't start until the evening," he explained. "Do you want to tour around Porto for a bit?"

I took him up on his offer without hesitation. We all got in the car and off we went.

Travelling through narrow and winding streets with centuries-old houses and ancient stately mansions on each side, the city that was founded in the early 10th century reminded me of Lisbon in many ways. The cobblestone roads, the magnificent churches, the fortresses and castles, as well as both cities being large international ports were all mutual characteristics.

In other ways, the northern city differed from its southern counterpart. It appeared to be older than

Lisbon-- perhaps because many of the old and grand edifices of Lisbon collapsed entirely in the Earthquake of 1755 -- and more European, possibly because it was further north. Additionally, the Moors were not expelled from Lisbon till 1147, two centuries after Porto returned to Christian hands. Therefore the Muslim influence was less evident up north.

But the multitude of cars squeezed randomly in each available spot, the coffee shops on each corner and the numerous *pastelarias* reassured me I was still in Portugal.

Our first destination was *praia da Boa Vista*, a stretch of sandy beaches, restaurants and cafés along the Atlantic Ocean. We walked along the wide cobblestone promenade for some time, enjoying the fresh air and the pleasant scent of the sea. We sat at a café and lingered over coffee (I drank my favorite lemon elixir of course), overlooking the waves that were breaking fiercely upon the occasional reefs.

Although very relaxing, the atmosphere in the north was slightly different than the one in the southern region. I pondered the puzzle for a while, trying to put my finger on the dissimilarity without success. Walking back, we followed a more crowded avenue, passing by some shops and stores.   It was then that I realized what the difference was.

The people walked ever so slightly faster. They drank their coffees a bit more rapidly. They seemed somewhat busier. It wasn't quite noticeable at first but it was indeed there, a nuance of a distinction. A Portuguese saying I once heard sprang to mind: "The residents of Porto work, the citizens of Braga pray while the inhabitants of Lisbon spend the money."

In light of my new conclusion, this saying was accurate, as the people of Porto did appear to be more industrious. On the other hand, the fact that Porto had the highest ratio in the world of Ferraris compared with its population hardly justified the part about Lisbon's inhabitants spending the money. I gave up trying to make sense out of it.

We traveled back along the coast until we reached the point where the Atlantic met the River Douro. Walking along the riverbank, a steep hill covered with quaint red-roofed buildings rose abruptly on our left, leaving enough room for a row of houses and a two-lane road. The old narrow sidewalk on the riverside of the street provided a continuous walking path by the water with a marvelous view.

The houses were replaced gradually by stores and soon we found ourselves in an old market where tiny shops were cramped one next to the other inside ancient buildings, the numerous narrow and colorful entrances forming a harmony in a unique way.

The sidewalk by the river widened ahead and was filled with stands of all sorts that offered assortments of fresh fish, mollusks and shellfish caught early that morning. Other stands also sold a variety of items from traditional clothes to handcrafted jewelry. The merchants were mostly sitting by their stands, too complacent to loudly advertise their merchandise. Still the market was bustling and full of activity.

Old Porto was beautiful and I fell in love with it. The varied styles of architecture, the mixture of serene and industrious atmospheres and the distinct feeling of a deep-rooted culture created an aura of enchantment around the city. I had no doubt I would return for another visit soon.

We then drove toward Campo, a small town about ten kilometers east of Porto, where João lived. Following his directions with hesitation, I took a turn on a small dirt road which led us for about two kilometers down to a hidden nook of wilderness. The hills around us were covered with small trees and wild bushes. In the distance one could hear the Ferreira River which curved between the hills all the way down to the Douro.

It was a nature reserve, João said and added that sometimes he and his friends would go there and camp overnight. I was amazed that up north as well, just like in Cascais, wide tracts of wilderness existed only minutes away from the city.

As we approached the river, the vegetation grew wilder and thicker. A low building in shambles stood by the water, a decades-old ruin of a water mill. Along the bank, a group of rocks offered a knee-high passage to the other bank. The water was clear and fresh. The flow was fast but even. Further down, the river broke over several large boulders, forming a multitude of miniature waterfalls.

We climbed the hill ahead of us and reached the top, from where we could see the surrounding hills and the river path snaking in between. Bird chirps of various pitches and the sound of water cascading upon stone were the only indication of life and motion around me. I stood there for a while, enjoying yet another one of those little heavens Portugal abounds in.

We headed back along a vague path, surrounded by large moss-covered rocks, thick pine trees and low wild shrubbery that completely covered the ground. A quarter of an hour later we were in João's home. His mother and young sister quickly prepared a small snack for us of bread, cheese and fruit. Sitting in his kitchen and eating my sandwich, I wondered at how hospitable my friend and his family were.

The hospitality of the people in the north is in fact known all over Portugal. They are the best hosts one can find in the country, I was told often, unless one attempted to criticize their soccer team. I was advised that this touchy and explosive subject was best left undiscussed.

The skies announced evening was slowly approaching and so we made our way to João's grandparents' house for the family's *São João* dinner. At first I felt awkward, as if imposing on my friend, but he insisted we come along and made both Teresa and me very welcome. His family made us feel just as welcome and amazingly treated us as family. I was overwhelmed at their friendliness and open-heartedness. They hardly knew me and didn't know Teresa at all.

The table was set on the wide patio, a number of chairs arranged around in the vicinity. Kids were playing in the yard while João's uncle was supervising the action at the grill. Members of the family were constantly moving around, bringing things out from the kitchen and arranging for this and that. Our plates were constantly filled with food and we found ourselves being urged to eat by all the mothers of the family.

Now, since I touched upon a subject near and dear to my heart – food – let me elaborate a bit about our meal. As mentioned before, sardines are at their best during the months of summer and so even in Porto I found these thin, short fish lying on the grill, getting a "sun tan." The distinct aroma of sardines getting grilled is unmistakable. Generous slices of meat were cooking beside the sardines.

A salad of fresh tomatoes, lettuce and grilled green peppers, covered with olive oil and tiny pieces of onions, the usual salad eaten with sardines, made for an excellent side dish which I began eating while waiting for the meat. Two perfectly grilled sardines arrived shortly on my plate and I was in business. The meal was finalized with a fruit salad for dessert.

Besides being occupied with the contents of their plates, the family members were always involved in a lively conversation of some sort. João's sister and cousin were both dressing up for the costume contest which was part of the festivities later on that evening in the village.

Elena, João's girlfriend and Ze, another friend of his, joined us and all five of us squeezed into my small Fiat. It was time to go to Porto for *noite de São João,* Saint João's night celebration. Armed with a large inflatable plastic hammer that I was told I would need, we made our way to the large city.

Parking was a slight problem and it took driving around for twenty minutes till we found a spot. After a long walk we arrived at the riverside street where we had been earlier that day. Whereas I thought it was crowded before, it was jam-packed now. Thousands of people filled the street.

"Tonight everybody walks to the Matosinhos' ocean beach, lights up bonfires and lingers around for an hour or two, and then walks back. This is the tradition." João explained.

"How long is the walk over there?" I asked innocently.

"Hmm, about fifteen kilometers each way."

I got exhausted at the mere thought and told him there was no reason to follow the tradition completely that night and that a few kilometers would suffice. I had already driven three hundred kilometers that morning as well as climbed the hills of Campo. He agreed with a smile. His girlfriend had to take an exam in school the next day anyway.

A light bump on my head made me turn around in alarm. A young girl stood there giggling mischievously, holding a plastic hammer in her hand. Seeing my big hammer, her eyes widened and she scurried away.

"It has been a tradition of decades to celebrate São João with these plastic hammers," Teresa explained to me, obviously aware of this odd and harmless practice.

It didn't serve any purpose other than entertainment. Most plastic hammers were about a foot long while mine was perhaps three feet long. It should be enough to protect all of us, I thought.

Prepared for the worst, I soon found out it wasn't as bad as I thought it would be. I must have been banged a thousand times on the head and only once or twice did it hurt, mainly because I tried to escape and the hammer landed unintentionally on my ear.

It was a strange game but I soon got into its spirit. People of all ages from little kids to elders, carried colorful plastic hammers of all sizes and shapes. I learned it was customary to wait a moment once you hit someone for him to turn around and retaliate. It was almost like the *beijinhos*, I reflected. I often had people hit me and linger around in front of me for their reward.

The little kids were especially struck with awe whenever they saw my hammer. It was sometimes taller than they and was definitely the biggest one around. As soon as they would see it coming down – and I would try to lift it higher in the air first for a better effect – they froze in their places and goggled at its rapid approach upon their small heads. I would then bow down to receive my "penalty" and they would joyfully strike with their little hammers and carry on their way.

The city was bathing in a million lights in honor of its Saint and traditional Portuguese music sounded from balconies and cafés. People were swaying in their places around specially constructed stages to the sounds of folklore melodies sung by street artists. Others were feasting upon the sardines to their heart's content in small improvised restaurants. There were no diet-watchers around, I observed.

Often, a score of teenagers holding hands would run past us following their leader in a "train," weaving through the numerous jovial pedestrians. My only guess was that they wanted to arrive at the beach first. And then when I saw a group running the other way, I ran out of guesses. It seemed that the only likely reason for their strange behavior was just to have fun.

A noisy explosion sounded above us. It was midnight, and a magnificent fireworks display began above us. The ever-moving stream of people came to a halt only once that evening for about ten minutes while the colorful and bright illuminations lighted up the skies. The show ended with a spectacular and deafening grand finale, to the cheers of all spectators. The flow restarted at once, never to halt again till the morning.

I noticed quite early in the evening that with all the thousands of people in the streets, some of them rather drunk, there were practically no fights or accidents. I was amazed at that phenomenon. In many countries, people get drunk and violent during such festivities, keeping squads of policemen busy. On São João, some roving policemen were strategically posted, but most of them lounged at their corners for the majority of the evening. Most Portuguese hate violence and know how to party without being party-wreckers.

I was about to land my huge inflatable hammer on an old man's bald head when suddenly out of nowhere, he thrust forward a large plant he was carrying and shook its flowers in my face. It smelled of garlic! I jerked my head back and sneezed, dropping my weapon in the process.

The elder smiled slyly and carried on his way while my friends were chuckling at my expense. I demanded to know what it was.

"It's a garlic thing," Elena replied with a smile. "It was the entire plant, roots and all. That is part of the São João celebration. You don't attempt to strike with your hammer anyone who carries a garlic thing!"

Great, now they tell me. Traces of garlic odor still lingered on me for a few minutes, and thereafter I used my hammer more cautiously. Although outnumbered by the plastic hammers, these garlic things were highly noticeable. As tall as five feet, their green thick stem wiggling above in the air, they stood out from the crowd with ease.

At the top of the plant was the light-blue crown that gave off the strong smell. At the bottom were the white roots which served as the handle. Although I never managed to (or desired to) identify the exact type of plant it was, it was certainly from the *Allium* genus.

At times the garlic bearers attempted to "bless" me with their plants without any reason or warning. I resignedly admitted eventually that the garlic thing was far more effective than my sizeable plastic hammer. All one had to do was carry the feared vegetable and nobody but garlic freaks would bother one, while one retained the option of bestowing the garlic-like fragrance upon the person of one's choice.

After an hour of walking with still another hour to go before reaching the ocean, we decided to turn back. That was easier said than done, as we now had to go against the flow. Luckily, on the right side of the street was a tiny stream of people on their return journey and we quickly joined in.

Around two in the morning, a special show began in a large square not too far from the *Ponte Dom Luis I*, an impressive double-decker iron bridge that spanned the river. The show featured well-known Portuguese songs of past and modern times. The square was packed with spectators who joined the singers often, loudly singing along. Couples cuddled to the sound of a *fado* song about love and later on danced to the rhythm of Portuguese pop music.

After a few songs that my friends were particularly fond of, we carried on our way. At a corner of two ancient streets outside a small bar, one of the customers was singing popular songs without a microphone, accompanied by the bar owner and his guitar. They were quite good and we stopped beside the other passerbys who formed a semi-circle around them and clapped merrily to the beat.

I reluctantly left the scene of the celebration, feeling very cheerful and happy. As we walked back to the car, I cogitated about the Portuguese way of enjoying life. They enjoy festivities in the same fashion they carry out their daily routines at work: unhurried, relaxed and peaceful

João's home was empty upon our return. His parents and little sister were celebrating in one of the local cafés and wouldn't be back till later, he said. He offered for us to stay there for the night, but I declined politely. There is a fine line between being a good guest and a burden, even in the case of the excellent northern hospitality, and I didn't want to cross that line.

We thanked him profusely for the enjoyable time we had that day and promised to keep in touch. Even as I was getting into the car, João was asking me if I was sure we didn't need some supplies for the way. After many warm good-byes, Teresa and I eventually started on our way back south.

Motoring along the *auto-estrada,* the glittering stars hanging above us in the spacious dark skies, I reached the conclusion that indeed there was no substitute to being happy and enjoying the company of other people. No one under the influence would ever reach the state of joy and happiness that I had witnessed in these Portuguese celebrations. So why try to artificially get high when all you need is a few Saints, sardines and garlic things?

Oh, and by the way, João's little sister won the costume contest.

Chapter 10
BUSY DOING NOTHING IN THE ALENTEJO

Welcome to the stress-free and sleepy region of the Alentejo. Set south of the river Tejo and north of the Algarve, stretching from the Atlantic Ocean over to the Spanish border, this spacious and magnificent mixture of plains and rolling hills is the sanctuary for the tired and the weary, as well as the scenic paradise for those seek to explore nature and wilderness.

My interest in the Alentejo was first stirred when I was watching a commercial on television one day. The first picture was of an old man sitting down in the shade of an older house, his hands and chin resting on his walking cane. It was late morning and the sun was baking everything in sight.

Suddenly a young boy riding his bicycle passed across the way and slowed down in front of the elder.

"*Bom dia, tio Manel*!" cried the youngster cheerfully in greeting and sped off to disappear in the background.

The old man did not even twitch.

The afternoon had passed and evening was approaching. The man was still slouched in the same position. Unexpectedly, as if realizing he had been spoken to, he responded.

"*Boa tarde*!" he said to the thin air where earlier the passer-by had paused to greet him.

Another humorous commercial followed, in which a traffic helicopter was scouting the skies above the Alentejo countryside.

"Yes, folks, we have a large traffic jam across the Bridge this afternoon," said the commentator excitedly. "I would strongly suggest to use the side roads whenever possible."

His voice faded out and the camera focused on a large herd of cows dawdling along the small and narrow bridge, their blank expressions filling the screen, and then moved on to show their herder taking his afternoon nap on a nearby bench.

It was at that instant when I realized it was THE place for me. An outpost as remote and distant as possible in the Alentejo was exactly what I needed, I rationalized, where life and its bugbears – schedules, tasks and conversations – were kept to the absolute minimum.

With vacation from life in mind, I set out on my way. As I was leaving the urban areas, driving south on the freeway from Lisbon, I could already sense the tenseness ebbing away. It felt as if a heavy load was lifting off my shoulders.

A short transfer from the freeway onto a state road in the Setúbal area, marked where one left civilization and approached cultivation. Passing along the River Sado's estuary, the densely populated regions made way for low agricultural hills while narrow roads replaced the wide highways.

The color of the vegetation was gradually changing from the bright and lively green around Lisbon and Setúbal to deeper green and even beige-tinted fields of wheat and corn. Occasionally, large tracts of sunflowers would dazzle the traveler with their vividly yellow petals.

As I was progressing south, short and peculiar trees began to appear sporadically across the fields. The lower part of the trunk was thinner and reddish-brown while the upper part, on up from where the tree was branching off, was thicker and grayish.

Stopping to take a closer look, I recognized it to be the famous cork tree. Portugal produces more than half of the world's cork (130,000 tons per year.) The biggest and best cork oaks are found mainly south of Lisbon (the Alentejo and Algarve regions) more in the coastal zones than inland. The Algarve cultivates tourism as its main industry whereas the Alentejo is one of the main cork-producing centers worldwide.

The gray bark, the cork, has to be peeled off expertly leaving the inside trunk unscathed; a delicate skill passed on from father to son. A bad gash will permanently damage the future growth and cork yield of the tree. Once stripped, it can take up to ten years for a new layer of cork to grow.

Its many valuable properties have put cork at the top of the materials list for many industries. It is an excellent insulator of sound as well as temperature and moisture. Its uses span a wide range from dartboards to protective capsules for transporting radioactive isotopes.

Thus far no other material, synthetic or natural, has been found to be able to seal wine bottles and still allow the precious liquid inside to "breathe" and mature through the years, as cork does. And in that respect, cork has been of supreme importance to the world. Surely a global catastrophe would take place should Portugal's cork workers take a collective vacation. What would Man do without wine?

Therefore, every cork tree has been well cared for and numerous laws have been passed for the conservation and protection of the cork tree.

Following N-120 southwest, a hilly plateau provided a different collection of impressive panoramas. Shrubs and large eucalyptus trees dotted the hillsides while smaller greenery had rooted itself sparsely in between.

The enthusiasm and zeal for growth which plants in other areas of Portugal possessed, was lacking in this region. Overall, it seemed the Alentejo's atmosphere of relaxation and sluggishness affected even the vegetation.

I carried on past Sines south to Cercal. The hills slowly flattened to a wide plain with a variety of vegetation, from miniature forests to large pastures where the occasional cow and sheep grazed. The layers of stress were peeling off me in rapid succession the deeper I went into the countryside.

Taking the N-390 and then a minor side road, I arrived in short order to Villa Nova de Milfontes. It was a small and lovely collection of brightly-painted picturesque houses arranged along the narrow and curving streets. The main road featured a few restaurants and inns, as well as some grocery shops and a convenience store.

I checked in at a small hostel by the beach and went up to unpack. The room's balcony doors were open, revealing a breathtaking view of a serene bay. The towering cliffs rose abruptly near the water, leaving a narrow golden strip of sand around the inlet.

In the distance, the Atlantic waves were breaking against the shoals where bay met ocean, their repetitive but not quite rhythmic sounds instilling a serene quality in the air. I sat down on the plastic recliner and rested there for several hours. At first the calmness that prevailed all things, inanimate and alive alike, was somewhat irritating. I kept looking around for something to do. Not being very successful at that, I simply did nothing and let the adrenaline wash out of my system.

It was getting late and the quiet street turned darker, its few lampposts waking up with the arrival of twilight. There was a peaceful quietude all around and besides the infrequent passing cars, the only other sound was of the far away waves.

When I arrived in Portugal from the States, I noticed the unique quality of Portugal as a relaxation heaven. But now, sitting and enjoying the idleness, I quickly formed the opinion that the same difference existed between the rest of Portugal and the Alentejo.

Reluctantly I got up from my seat. My stomach was insisting it was dinner time. Off I went up the street till I reached a quasi-square situated before an old castle. Creepers nearly hid the walls of the little fort, and at first I had some trouble identifying what was under the green blanket. A narrow wooden drawbridge spanned the deep moat. It was a small classy hotel, I found out.

The square was, judging by the number of people sitting and strolling about, the meeting place of the village. Walking across its mosaic pavement, I pondered the dilemma of this typically Portuguese form of paving which dates back to the Roman rule. It is difficult to walk on, time consuming to lay and requires periodic maintenance, but it is the traditional way of surfacing sidewalks in Portugal. Its aesthetic and traditional values, in my opinion, outweigh by far the inconveniences. What would the square look like had they just covered up stones with cement, dotted it with some parking meters and converted the old castle into a fast-food restaurant?

Shuddering at the possibility, I decided to enjoy the current scenery while it lasted. I found an outside table in a small restaurant on the other side of the square overlooking the centuries-old view. I ate two toasted cheese sandwiches and lingered for a while over a *carioca de limão*. A couple of hours later, I was back at the hostel.

It had been a long and productive day, I reflected, having accomplished many complete and utter nothings. After such a hard day's work, I surely deserved a good night's rest. With the window half open, I fell asleep to the background hiss of the distant surf breaking upon reef and sand.

I woke up to the cheerful cock-a-doodle-doos of a rooster right outside my window. I attempted to cover my ears with the pillow to no avail. The bird carried on with its persistent crowing, as if it had been given the specific task of waking me up. I eventually staggered out of bed, ready to shoot the darned creature. But then it dawned on me that that was too much work. I washed and put on a pair of swimming trunks and a T-shirt instead.

After a light breakfast, beach towel and sunglasses in hand, I sauntered across the street and shuffled along the sand to a strategically advantageous position, where the sun would find me but the wind wouldn't. The golden sand was scattered with various bird tracks. The water was blue and calm. The sun was slowly warming up. I lay on the towel and put on my sunglasses.

The beach got more populated as the hours passed by but since it was only May, it never actually got as crowded as it does in July and August. Kids were playing soccer in the distance, dogs were interrupting the game and the parents were playing dead on top of their beach towels like myself. The immediate area around my sandy "lair" remained relatively vacant, allowing me to doze off again and again.

Around two o'clock, after a long argument with my limbs and muscles which thought they were included in the vacation, I made it to my feet. Suddenly, walking appeared to be an arduous task. In fact, any activity other than breathing seemed to fall in the category of hard work.

Eating was not hard work, my stomach protested. And in the Alentejo that couldn't be truer. After about ten minutes of driving south on the narrow N393, I made it to "*Restaurant O Cruzamento*", a small inconspicuous establishment on the left side of the road.

The homey restaurant, consisting of a medium-sized dining room and a similar-sized coffee shop, was of plain design. In the café section, six or seven elders were discussing the weather, several bottles of wine and numerous coffee cups standing empty on their table. A quiet couple occupied a table nearby. The wooden furniture was sturdy and coarse, the dining table covered with a large paper tablecloth. The approaching waiter was moving too fast for my taste, I noticed with a smile.

Wisely, I ordered a small portion of *ensopado de peixe* – a dish between fish soup and stew, knowing how the quantities of the entrés got out of hand in this region. Soon arrived a basket of thick Alentejo bread, a bowl of fat olives and a small plastic holder with fresh white cheese inside. I turned the plastic holder over the bread plate and let the soft cheese slide out. Sprinkled with lots of pepper and a bit of salt, the cheese was delicious.

Time crawled by as I consumed the appetizers. Half an hour later my *ensopado de peixe* arrived in a large cooking pot. I looked at it with disbelief. If that was the small portion, what was a large one?

The pot contained an entire fish cut into four, potatoes and slices of bread. It seemed physically impossible to finish such a gigantic portion. In the Alentejo, I concluded, no matter how hard you try to avoid it, you would always be full when you leave a restaurant.

Well, my stomach didn't particularly object to the idea and so I got to work. The fish was tender and tasty, the potatoes well cooked and the soup delicious. I was unable to finish the portion, and the waiter came by anxiously to inquire as to the quality of the food. I assured him the only problem was that my stomach had reached its limits.

It was a simple, hearty and inexpensive meal, served in a friendly and peaceful environment, characteristic of most Alentejo restaurants. I topped it off with a *carioca de limão*, staring out the window for long periods of time between sips

I returned to Milfontes and sat out on my balcony for several hours, watching the distant waves as if hypnotized. Evening arrived and I ended up watching the beautiful sunset against the Atlantic horizon, the glorious golden-reddish fireball melting slowly into the water.

Night was setting in so I paid another visit to the restaurant overlooking the old castle to have a light dinner. I retired close to midnight, having done absolutely nothing the entire day and having enjoyed every moment of it. Yes, I let out a deep sigh of content; this was what the Alentejo was all about.

The next morning I loaded up my car and left on my journey to the other side of the Alentejo. I had to ascertain, for the sake of my readers, whether the eastern parts of the region offered the same quality of life as the western coast. After studying the map carefully, I established there was no other option but to take the scenic route along the small side roads and through the numerous tiny villages – there was simply no other way there.

The vegetation along the road was ever changing. Olive groves became dense agricultural tracts, which suddenly transformed into grazing pastures, shortly to be replaced by barren unplowed soil. Vineyards of different shapes and sizes came into view repeatedly, often situated right along the road. Cork oaks frequented the landscape, their reddish trunks catching one's eye at once.

Passing through a small village, I stopped by the main (and only) square to appreciate the view of an old church. It was two stories high, and its walls were made of ancient stones. Its large wooden double doors were wide open, welcoming anyone who wished to wander in. In front of it, at the square, four bright red benches were situated around a small fountain -- the center of the square. The contrast of the gray stone pavement and the green treetops against the red seats and the pure white walls of the nearby houses created an aura of antiquity.

If it weren't for the electrical poles, I would have surely concluded I had traveled back in time.

Four older men occupied the bench closest to the church, their overall image similar but each face expressing a different world. Sitting there, *boné* hats protecting the top of their heads from the sun, each appeared to be engrossed in his own intense meditation.

The one on the right corner, wearing a brown and black checkered shirt and a tan *boné*, was looking straight ahead. The older man beside him, in a bronze-colored sweater, had his hat so far down his forehead there was no way of telling where he was looking. The shortest and oldest, sitting in the middle, had the sleeves of his long blue shirt rolled up and was watching the stranger (me), while the heavyset man on the left was staring into space.

In the background, a youngster was riding her bicycle around while several women were watching her. A car passed by occasionally. A dozen ancient scooters were parked across the street near a café. It seemed that those scooters, probably older than those riding them, were the favorite mode of transportation in the Alentejo. Using a mixture of gasoline and oil for fuel and having a small motor, they were inexpensive and simple to use.

The heavyset fellow finally spoke and the eldest commented with an unhurried shake of the head. A period of silence ensued. Next, the man on the right said something to which, after a pause, the older man replied. I realized I was watching an argument in slow motion. I adored the sight: no signs of heated discussions or loud conversations, just a calm and peaceful debate.

Following the road out of the village, I found myself at an intersection between two deserted roads that separated several pieces of land. On the far side of the crossing, a small olive tree stood between two rows of bench-like concrete seats painted white.

Beneath the tree, five men in *Alentejano* attire, *boné*s and all, were seated, two in the shade and the others basking in the sun. One of them had a small chair while the others were perched along the white solid bench. An old motor scooter with a wooden box attached behind the seat was parked a few yards away, while a small tan dog of unknown breed lay on the warm earth near the men. The man on the left talked while the three in the middle were listening. The man on the far right was solely eavesdropping, it seemed, as he sat at the far right corner of the bench, detached, looking blankly ahead.

I approached them asking for directions, which they kindly gave me.

"If you don't mind me asking," I added, " why are you people sitting here in the middle of nowhere?" The man, who was talking earlier and proved to be the spokesman of the group, considered the question for a moment before answering.

"Because it's for free and away from the noise of the village," came the reply. The rest smiled in agreement.

"And is the dog yours?" I asked, petting the little creature.

"No. He doesn't belong to anyone these days, he is retired." We all laughed together and the dog wagged its tail unhurriedly. It was true. The dog behaved like a true *Alentejano*.

I thanked them and they resumed their discussion concerning a fair being held at a nearby village. The scene seemed so ridiculous at first – five adults sitting by the roadside under a tree, talking about who knows what for hours. But then, it made sense. Why sit in a crowded café and pay, when you can enjoy the view of nature and the fresh air for hours on end at a corner of a deserted intersection, without paying one *escudo*?

With this piece of Alentejo wisdom, I waved goodbye and drove away. Passing through the large village of Odemira, I stopped at a lovely *miradouro* – a typical spot where one can take a break and enjoy the view. Located on the side of the hill and overlooking Odemira and the River Mira, it consisted of a set of five concrete pillars painted bright white, arranged in a semi-circle. Each pillar extended out at the bottom to create a seat of sorts on each side. Narrow tiles made of orange-brown clay which were embedded in the seat one next to each other, combined into a "cushion". Above the pillars, a wide framework of dark wood, covered with climbing plants, comprised the *miradouro's* roof.

All on its own, serving no other purpose, it was merely an aesthetic structure designed to simply please the travelers along the road. I sat there for a while admiring the view, putting the *miradouro* to use. More cars stopped and soon the *miradouro* was a crowded location.

Several incidents highlighted my otherwise routine journey, which I feel are worth mentioning. I have seen the triangular road sign with an outline of a cow in its center many a time in my life, but had always taken little heed. Usually, there wasn't even a single animal in sight.

But after an hour or so of travelling through the changing Alentejo scenery, I nearly got run over by an entire herd of cattle. I was driving down a narrow and serpentine road when suddenly I could see nothing but large brown cows. They weren't passing near the road or beside it, but were actually walking along it on the asphalt lanes.

Not having any choice, I braked hard to a halt. The cows were not concerned at all with the appearance of this strange object in their path. These large beasts whose shoulders were higher than my car's rooftop, simply went around the car and carried on past me. For a moment I was afraid they might try to horn my Fiat, but they proved to be friendly and tame. The herder was slowly following the last cow and judging by his shuffle, could have easily been mistaken for one of the herd.

Later on, I also came across a similar event but with sheep. These small creatures that were occupying my lane, were constantly attempting to disperse in different directions, but their old shepherd was lucky enough to have a secret weapon with which to keep them in line. A small dog, perhaps a foot tall, assisted him in his task and chased the stray sheep back to the flock.

And finally, just when I thought I had seen it all, a young man riding an old motor scooter passed by, a bale of hay twice his size occupying the back seat of his tiny vehicle.

Throughout the trip, I found nothing but a calm and quiet lifestyle. People worked, but they were never in a hurry. People enjoyed the luxuries of modern living while at the same time keeping to their traditions. They enjoyed the food, and large quantities of it at that, and drank a lot of wine. Life was good and simple.

So far, the Alentejo had continued to display all of the merits I had found so prevalent along its beaches.

It was getting close to lunchtime and as I passed through each village, a distinctly different and savory aroma of home cooking filled my nostrils, causing my stomach to stir each time. I finally gave in to temptation (how could one not?) and stopped at the next local café.

A common snack in Portugal with the unique capability of keeping hunger away for hours is the *empada,* a cup-like pastry filled with pieces of chicken meat and sausage. Normally it is served without being heated up, though I personally prefer it warm.

I consumed two of these warmed up pastries, the tasty mix of the meat and crusty casing satisfying my appetite. I then drove across the final stretch to Monsaraz, which was an uphill winding road of about three kilometers.

Close to the Spanish border, Monsaraz is a fortified village with a castle that commands a view of the surrounding thirty-kilometer radius or thereabouts. It is a grand and impressive edifice, which has been modified, damaged and reconstructed countlessly since its original construction over eight centuries ago.

Regardless of its past history, it is now a part of the Alentejo. It came as no surprise that right at the gate, sitting along a stone bench, was a group of older *Alentejanos* equipped with their *bonés*, slowly arguing about an unknown but nonetheless important subject. I made a mental note of the sight. Surely it would be useful when forming my retirement plans in the future.

Within the fortified stone walls, a lovely maze of small and large buildings revealed itself. Some of the cobblestone streets were so narrow they didn't allow for passage of cars. The attractive white facades of the houses, their red roofs jutting out from above, were of different shapes and sizes, and offered numerous views of pretty doors, gates and windows.

In the heart of the village, a solemn and desolate square about twenty yards wide was situated in front of a grand church. The stately building that stood beside the church served in the past as Town Hall and Courthouse, later on to become the Monsaraz prison. It was in this house that the exceptional 15th century wall painting 'Earthly Justice' was discovered not too long ago.

A few elders were unhurriedly walking up the street. A woman was sweeping around her doorstep nearby. Several stray goats were roaming about. Whereas centuries ago Monsaraz was the site of untold number of battles, sieges and rushes, it was now a location for a quiet and peaceful village.

I left reluctantly as the sun was setting in the west, content with my findings that even on this side of the Alentejo, the same rule is followed as regards to speed, stress and heated arguments – avoid them at all costs.

On my way back I stopped at the *"Bar Alentejano"* restaurant in Montemor-o-Novo for dinner. I entered through the small bar section at the front, and arrived at the dining room. Perhaps ten sizeable wooden tables were arranged neatly about the room, the matching wooden chairs heavy but comfortable.

Fine wood paneling ran across each wall up to waist level and gave the room a homey atmosphere. The rest was heavily yet tastefully decorated with intriguing artifacts of the Alentejo tradition. An entire array of antique agricultural tools, from small knives used for pruning vines to large wooden rakes, hung across one wall. The opposite wall was an exhibit of many items connected with bull fighting, including capes, *bandarilhas*, a pair of wooden stirrups as well as some of the traditional clothing. Pictures and posters of famous bulls, horses and bullfighters were also in the collection.

I ordered a *gaspacho alentejano*, cold vegetable soup, and a small portion of *ensopado de borrego*, lamb cooked in sauce.

The soup arrived in a large bowl and to my astonishment had several ice cubes floating amid the raw sliced tomatoes, cucumbers, green peppers and olives. A few pieces of bread were also added in. It had a unique savory taste and was very refreshing. A few drops of olive oil and oregano put the final touches to this superb dish.

My jaw must have dropped when I saw the approaching main course. It consisted of a large ceramic pot where potatoes and slices of bread were floating in the sauce, while another platter carried the large pieces of meat decorated with tomato and lettuce.

As usual, the mere sight of the Alentejo culinary preparations made one hungry.

The tender lamb, soaked in its sauce together with the potatoes and the bread, made for a paradisiacal combination. I didn't even attempt to finish it this time, but resignedly ordered a *carioca de limão* to signal the end of the meal. The waiter raised his eyebrows, observing the half-full pot. I smiled and complimented the chef on his creation, which eased the waiter's mind.

I let infinity pass before reaching the bottom of the teacup. It was evident that the entire region answered to the same forces and followed the same rules.

And if one desired to get away from it all and unwind for a while, I would strongly recommend to leave one's portable computer, cellular phone, beeper and friends behind, bring a checkered shirt and a *boné* hat along, and get lost somewhere in the Alentejo.

Upon my arrival home, a distinct feeling of being out of place stirred within me. The urban noise, hurry and action that I had always adored were not as attractive suddenly.

It took me a few days to readjust to city life again. However, to this date, a momentary relapse still occurs every now and then, and I revert back to the sluggish habits I acquired in those three lazy days in the Alentejo.

I had obviously caught the contagious Alentejo flu. And everybody knows there is no known cure for that.

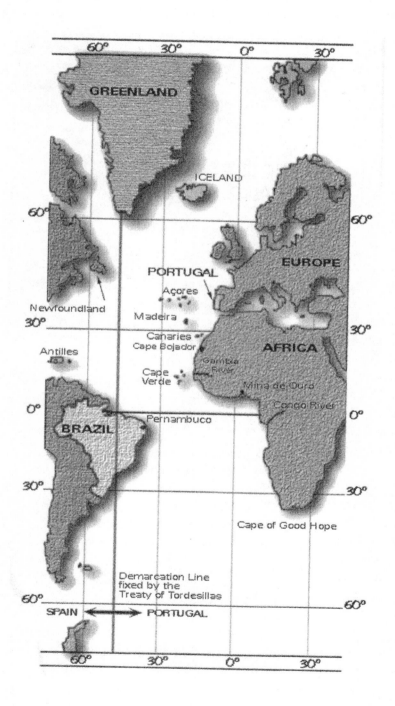

Chapter 11
THE LION, THE EAGLE AND THE TIGER

Portugal has a very rich history. I've been to so many castles, seen so many types of architecture and heard so much about the discoverers that one day I decided to study a bit of the history of the country I was visiting and find out what these were all about.

Probing through the complex, intricate and detailed history books, I eventually managed to come up with an orderly, simple analysis. It revolves around three personalities. The way I see it, they, much like the powerful symbols I have attached to them, are the central figures in Portugal's past.

Now, when it comes to history, my worst nightmare is the names of people and places. Latin or Greek names are often used in history books without explanation, and I am expected to instinctively know where each ancient Roman city is located today or which of the northern tribes resided along the Rhine in the fifth century. I have tried to refrain from subjecting my readers to the same treatment. For your reference, on the next page you will find a map of Portugal and the world with all the places I mention.

All right, ready?

The Chaotic Jungle

The name of the country itself originates from *Portus Cale,* the Latin name for the city of Porto. From there it evolved to *Portucale* and later on to Portugal.

In Julius Caesar's day, Lisbon was the center of Roman rule in Portuguese territory, the only city in the west with Roman rights. The chief concentration of Romans or Romanized settlements was in the valley of River Tejo and in the Algarve but there are innumerable remains of Roman culture all over Portugal, with more being discovered currently in the course of constructing Lisbon's subway.

At that time, *Portucale* was a quiet and relatively peaceful region.

On the last day of 406 AD, four barbarian tribes from Germany moved to the Iberian Peninsula. These were the Swabians, Alans and two groups of Vandals. After engaging in numerous wars the Vandals and Alans headed south and crossed the Strait of Gibraltar over to Africa.

The Swabians were the only Germanic people left in the Peninsula until the Visigoths, a large tribal kingdom that occupied Gaul began to rule Spain. Up to the year 711 several wars, battles and changes of territories occurred, but the Swabians and Visigoths still remained the sole rulers of the Iberian Peninsula.

In the year of 711, crossing the Strait of Gibraltar from North Africa, the Muslim invasion began. By 714 this new Muslim force occupied most of the Peninsula and remained there for several centuries. Moorish influence is to this date evident in the central and southern parts of Portugal (for example, 'Algarve' actually means 'the western land' in Arabic.)

The old Swabian territory remained in the hands of one house throughout the various conquests and conflicts. The barons of this territory were excluded from participating in the wars with the Muslims and continued governing their counties, Coimbra and Portucale, not undisturbed.

« map of Spain and Portugal»

The Visigothic leaders who still held against the Muslims in the far north began the Christian reconquest around 718. By 753, they reached as far as the middle of the Peninsula thus creating the kingdoms of Castile, Leon, Navarre and Galicia. In 1072, King Alfonso VI united the kingdoms under him and assumed the title of emperor. The counties of Portucale and Coimbra were now added to Galicia.

Around the year of 1095, the French noble Henry of Burgundy arrived in Portugal and after marrying Afonso VI's daughter, assumed the title of Count of Portugal, combining both Coimbra and Portucale into one county.

Count Henry died in 1112, leaving behind a young son of five, Afonso Henriques. The widowed mother ruled the county for over a decade. However, she was far from skilled in politics and her refusal to pay homage to Alfonso VII brought about his eventual invasion of Portugal in 1127.

The Lion

The Portuguese barons began to look to Afonso Heriques, who was now twenty, for leadership.

He quickly took matters into his own hands, aware of the mistakes his mother had made. He started exercising his authority and in July 1128, at the head of a group of barons, he faced his mother's army near Braga. Afonso Henriques was victorious. He captured his mother, expelled her to Galicia and assumed his father's title, the Count of Portugal.

In 1135 Alfonso VII, the heir to the Spanish Emperor title, convoked a great assembly to confirm his title and to obtain homage from his subordinates. Afonso Henriques did not attend it.

Next Afonso Henriques advanced and defeated the rulers north of the River Minho, a section of the county that was taken away from his mother by the Spanish invasion of 1127. This brought the emperor to the scene and he ordered the Galician barons to make war on Portugal. But negotiations were made and an agreement of sorts was reached.

Afonso Henriques was brave enough to make these bold moves in the face of a fierce enemy such as the collective kingdoms of Spain, but not stupid enough to open a full war on Castile.

In July 1139 the young count won the famous victory over the Muslims in a place called Oric or Ouric. Its definite location has not been established, but most probably it was near Santarém. Though the battle was on a modest scale, it marks the birth of the kingdom of Portugal. According to myth, Afonso Henriques had a vision while on the battlefield in which God entrusted him with leading his people toward an autonomous kingdom.

When the enemy fled, Portugal acquired a new conquest and a new king. Count Afonso Henriques began using the royal title and was hereafter referred to as "King of Portugal", though not officially referred to as king by the Holy See till 1179.

The new king began expanding his domain on a large scale. In 1147, he captured the city of Santarém (then occupied by Muslims.) Two months later, a large fleet of 164 ships and 13,000 crusaders arrived at Porto in on their way to the Holy Land. With much persuasion and diplomatic talk, he managed to convince the crusaders to assist him in attacking Muslim-held Lisbon. The crusaders who were English, German and Flemish were not easy to control. Yet he did.

Once all the ships and the Portuguese army arrived in Lisbon, Afonso Henriques organized the siege. After several weeks, the besieged asked for a truce. The crusaders, who had been promised the spoils of the city and suspecting the King would accept a tribute and leave, caused an uproar. King Afonso calmed them down by threatening he would indeed leave the field if there was any further commotion. The crusaders renewed their oaths to the King and order was restored.

The siege lasted for seventeen weeks and finally on 25 October 1147 the besiegers entered the city and much violence occurred over a period of three days. The Muslims surrendered, handed over their possessions and departed.

Having conquered Lisbon, Afonso Henriques isolated Sintra which then promptly surrendered. The Muslims abandoned the forts of Palmela and Portugal's boundaries now nearly reached Évora. He quickly organized and populated his newly conquered terrain with Portuguese citizens and monks from the north.

Occupying the city of Lisbon, King Afonso I was now equipped to launch an even stronger attack on the Muslims. Like a lion, he fought fearlessly and advanced across the south of Portugal relentlessly for four decades, all the while defending his realm and the people with remarkable ability.

On 23 May 1179, Pope Alexander III issued the bull officially confirming Afonso Henriques' royal title and his rights to all of his conquests and proclaiming him as King Afonso I of Portugal.

When King Afonso I died on 6 December 1185, Portugal's boundaries were not unlike today's excluding the southernmost strip of the Algarve. He was nearly eighty years of age and had reigned for fifty-seven. No depiction of him has survived but per the legend he was of a gigantic stature, Herculean strength and had a flowing beard.

King Afonso I's vision of an independent country was so strong that since his time, Portugal's boundaries have changed very little. His determined battle for and attainment of self-government inspired his heirs as well as the Portuguese people to defy foreign rulers with ferocity ever since.

* * *

The successive heirs to the Portuguese crown continued expelling the Muslims but not as rapidly. It was only in 1249, under King Afonso III, that the rest of the Algarve was conquered.

So far so good, it seemed. The Muslim enemy was sent back to where it came from and the young kingdom was making progress in resettling the newly conquered regions. But they weren't left to rest on their laurels.

Portugal was nearly united with Castile under one king in 1383, when the only heiress married the Castilian king. When he attempted to claim his right to the Portuguese throne, he was countered by João of Avis, a bastard son of the deceased Portuguese king Pedro I.

Civil conflicts ensued, with some favoring the Castilian king and some João of Avis. In March 1385 an assembly of the people officially elected João as king, forming a new Portuguese dynasty– the House of Avis.

The Castilian takeover attempt was derailed, but not without a fight. Through an alliance with England, Portugal won the battle of Aljubarrota on the fourteenth of August 1385 against the Castilian army and thus secured its independence from Spain for another two centuries.

The Eagle

King João I married an English princess, Philippa of Lancaster, in 1387 and had six children: five princes and one princess. The eldest, Dom Duarte inherited the throne. The one we are most interested in is named Dom Henrique.

Early in his life the young prince became educated with the ideals of the military Order of Christ of which he later became governor and administrator.

In 1415, the king conquered Ceuta of north Morocco thus establishing Portuguese maritime command over the waters between Portugal and Morocco. He then bestowed upon Dom Henrique the titles of Duke of Viseu and Governor of the Algarve.

Thus equipped with authority, the prince began his venture that would forever change world history.

Dom Henrique was a practical man. In my opinion he was a visionary as well, with an insight to the future, an ambition to forward the expansion of Christianity and a desire to advance nautical and navigational sciences. His ultimate dream was to reach India by sea and weaken the Muslim monopoly of spice trade from the Far East.

In Sagres, situated at the southwestern tip of Portugal, Dom Henrique established a unique navigator's school where he collected copies of all the maps, books and maritime manuals available at the time. He also invited the finest sea captains, cartographers and navigators of the world to join him in his court.

Sanctioned by his father, Dom Henrique set the exploration of the Atlantic Ocean into motion. Sailing aboard the *barcas,* Dom Henrique's captains and navigators began traveling west.

The first voyage from Dom Henrique's court to be recorded was in late 1418 or early 1419. The two Portuguese captains who headed the expedition, reported they had landed in an uninhabited island approximately a thousand kilometers southwest of Portugal which they had named Porto Santo. A year later they landed on the nearby island of Madeira, also uninhabited, and colonization began in 1420.

In 1427, the Islands of Azores, an archipelago stretching over 600 kilometers and located a third of the way across the Atlantic in the latitude just south of Lisbon, were officially discovered by another navigator sent by Dom Henrique. A few of the islands had been sighted before, evidenced by their appearance, though not exact in terms of location and size, on Portuguese maps in the 1300s.

Dom Henrique saw to the colonization of the new territory and soon the islands became bustling ports of call for the Portuguese merchants. He received a fifth of the total revenues from the Azores.

Then he began the exploration of the West African coast. Year after year he sent out ships in vain to pass the dreaded Cape Bojador (a Cape of the Western Sahara, about two hundred kilometers south of the Canary Islands) which was the end of the known world. Beyond lay, according to the myths, the Sea of Darkness and its boiling waters.

Finally, in the year of 1434, Gil Eanes, one of Dom Henrique's sea captains, successfully navigated past the cape and returned with the news that broke the naval superstition of those times. The first step to discovering the path to India was achieved.

The next step was the advent of the *caravela,* many of which were built in Dom Henrique's shipyards in Lagos (a port town in the Algarve.) About 25 meters long and carrying a crew of twenty and up to 80 tons of cargo, these double-masted, lateen-rigged boats were bigger, faster and easier to sail into the wind. The extensive use of this vessel quickly became a factor in the acceleration of the discoveries.

The improvement of navigational instruments was rapid in Dom Henrique's court and soon the navigation by the Pole star and the compass were aided by quadrants, astrolabes and celestial tables. The information gathered in each voyage was rapidly added to the maps by Dom Henrique's cartographers.

In 1438, Dom Henrique received a monopoly of trade with all lands he might discover.

Under Dom Henrique's direction, his navigators conducted a series of explorations along the West African coast and reached the Gambia River by 1446. Commercial sailors closely followed discoverers, and unfortunately the purchase of Moors and blacks by those merchant sailors soon became the highly profitable slave-trading business.

Dom Henrique did not attempt to confine the vast knowledge he had gathered nor exclude others from his activities. On the contrary, many foreign navigators, sea captains and squires were invited to his court and participated in the discoveries.

Dom Henrique wisely sent letters to various European thrones inviting their collaboration in his quest in Africa and offering to divide with them all profits. Each politely declined the kind offer and informed Dom Henrique that he may go ahead alone – they were quite ready to desist from all their rights.

He presented their responses to the Pope, Nicholas V, who in 1454, issued a Bull which stated "the conquest extending from Capes Nun and Bojador and all the coast of Guinea to the whole Orient is everlastingly and for all time the sovereign property of King Afonso V of Portugal..."

By his actions, he secured for Portugal the eastern route to India. In September 1460, shortly before his death, Sierra Leone was discovered which constitutes the final discovery voyage he sponsored.

Dom Henrique died in debt; all of the African trade could not generate enough funds to support his explorations.

After reading about Dom Henrique's life, I felt much awe for the man. Unlike the many kings and knights of his day, Dom Henrique successfully used intelligence and knowledge to lead Portugal in the direction that he wanted. His singleness of purpose and achievements had greatly contributed to the transition from the Medieval Age to the Renaissance.

And the Tiger

When King Afonso V's successor, João II, came to the throne in 1481, he took control of the African explorations and trade.

He at once enacted a new policy whereby confidentiality and secrecy were mandatory in his center of discoveries as well as in the shipyards. He enacted legislation that doubled pay for ship-builders and put any forest at his disposal should he need more wood to build new ships.

He invited many cartographers, astrologers and men of science who were not part of the court, to join him in the revival of Dom Henrique's quest. Having gone beyond the equator, with the Northern Star out of sight, navigation depended on sun height tables and latitude charts more then ever before. Mathematicians and navigators got together and produced the "*Regimento do Astrolabio*," the first elementary guide to navigation.

King João II managed to elicit papal Bulls threatening excommunication for those unlawfully traveling through the Portuguese territory. He passed laws against unauthorized trading in his dominion, stating that any poacher found should die and all his property be confiscated to the Crown.

Not only that but the local African tribes didn't

tolerate strangers other than perhaps the Portuguese, who attempted to form friendly alliances from the outset whenever they arrived at a new shore. In 1475 a Castilian pilot and thirty-five Flemish traders managed to sneak by Portuguese guard ships to Guinea in search for gold. They landed on a shore one night and there the inhabitants dined off the thirty-five Flemings.

Those who were not consumed by cannibals usually suffered a different, but not much better, fate. The King's ships sank many a foreign ship after relieving it of its goods. It was crystal clear that King João II was not a man to be trifled with.

Like a tiger, he knew when to strike at his enemies and eliminated them one by one with such trying patience that his friends revered him for his self-control. He had a unique ability to command men and had an entire network of loyal spies working for him inside and outside Portugal.

These informed him of several conspiracies shortly after he inherited the throne. The first was plotted by the mighty Duke of Bragança (a large duchy in the north of Portugal) who sought the help of Castile to overthrow him. The King waited months, all the while knowing the Duke's schemes, until he had conclusive evidence with which to arrest and execute him.

Following the Duke's public beheading, the Queen's older brother who had an eye on the throne, conspired against the King with a group of other lords. The King waited patiently, calmly ignoring two attempted assassinations, before he finally called in the conspirator and in the tower of his palace executed him with his own hands.

King João II was vicious toward his enemies but never failed to reward his supporters. He had a secret roll of honor that he kept to himself and was seen by his eyes only. There he wrote in the names of those who had served him well and should be remembered when a good occasion arose. As well, he compiled a list of the available men and their qualifications. Thus any need for filling a vacancy was not done by applications as usual but by the King's study of his secret register in private and the appointment of the most deserving.

His passion for justice won him the admiration of the people. He despised injustice or justice done with favors due to the status of the accused. Thus before the court, everyone was equal. He held paperwork and bureaucracy in contempt and paid attention only to petitions submitted in person.

He loved to ride though the streets every now and then to converse with the common men and women. And with that he won the heart of the people as well.

In my opinion he was the best king Portugal ever had. He considered his reign as a duty with the purpose of assisting the people, rather than ruling the people. Cunning and levelheaded, he transformed his small kingdom into the first modern empire. King João's only mistake as I see it, was not preparing his heir to inherit the powerful empire he had built.

Meanwhile, the discovery voyages continued. In 1474 or 1475 King João II had a fortified trading post erected in Mina de Ouro near the African gold mines to increase protection against intruders, converting the local African tribe to Christianity in the process. In 1482, Diogo Cão reached the River Zaire (or Congo) and visited the northern coast of Angola, forming close relations with the chief of the local tribe, eventually leading to the Manicongo tribe taking up the Christian faith.

And then came the theory that India could be reached from the west. A Florentine physician, Paolo Toscanelli, relayed the information to King João II that per calculations Marco Polo's Cipango (Japan) would be only 5,500 kilometers west of Portugal and the legendary Antillia only 1,500.

These figures seem to have not impressed the Portuguese, but it came to the notice of Christopher Columbus, a sea captain who had taken part in several discovery voyages. In 1481 or 1482, Columbus put forth a proposal to João II concerning the westward voyage.

The King passed Columbus on to his experts who had earlier dismissed Toscanelli's theory that India could be easily reached from the west. The frustrated Columbus, having gained no support for his plans in Portugal, moved to the Spanish court where he tried to enlist the Queen's assistance.

In 1488, Bartolomeu Dias, under King João's flag, doubled the African Cape of Good Hope. The route to India was wide open. It was now only a matter of time, as well as the construction of large enough ships to sustain the journey, before the Orient would be reached via the eastern route.

In April of 1492, Columbus managed to obtain the Spanish Crown's assistance and in August sailed out west. He returned a year later, with specimens of birds, plants and odd, copper-colored captives, believing he had discovered India. King João summoned him at once and interviewed him personally.

João II treated Columbus with the utmost respect and politeness despite Columbus' hints at the King's mistake for having turned him down. King João then informed the rulers of Spain that their advancement into Portuguese territory (since the land Columbus found was south of the Canaries and thus belonged, by the 1454 Papal decree, to Portugal) was highly against his liking. He at once began preparing a fleet to sail and claim the new territory.

The Spanish protested loudly and appealed to the Holy See who came out with a Bull proposing a meridian 100 leagues (roughly 480 kilometers) west of the Cape Verde Islands, stretching from Pole to Pole. This line would divide the world in half, giving any newly discovered lands to its east to Portugal and any newly found islands or continents to its west to Castile.

King João showed no interest in this Bull but continued the preparation of the fleet. The Castilians suggested a conference and Portugal agreed to delay the launching of the fleet for a period of seventy days. In the meanwhile Queen Isabel sent Columbus to "India" again for further explorations so as to better evaluate her position.

King João pressed the Castilians into negotiations

after the seventy-day period lapsed and refrained from sending out the westbound fleet. In the following months while out at sea exploring the Antilles, Columbus sent back encouraging reports that he had indeed found Japan.

King João sent ambassadors to the Castilian court with detailed instructions. Per records, he even predicted what the King and Queen of Spain would tell them and ensured they knew their exact responses. To the amazement of his messengers, the predicted statements of the Castilian rulers were accurate. They delivered their dictated responses as instructed and the result was the Treaty of Tordesillas in 1494.

The treaty resembled the earlier proposal of the Pope dividing the world between Castile and Portugal, but upon King João's insistence, placed the dividing line at 370 leagues (about 1770 kilometers) west of the Cape Verde Islands.

King João II died in October 1495, two years before the voyage of Vasco da Gama to India by the eastbound sea route, the first European to sail to and set foot in Calicut (Kozhikode of present times on the west coast of India.)

* * *

In 1497, with the beginning of the Inquisition in Portugal under Manuel I, all men of other faiths were ordered by the King to convert to Christianity or to leave the country. Many Jewish and Muslim scientists, mathematicians and chartmakers in his court traveled to other countries with their knowledge and skill (among these was the Jew Abraão Zacuto, the King's mathematician and astronomer who wrote the *Almanach Perpetuum*.)

For a short period at the beginning of the sixteenth century, King Manuel was considered the wealthiest ruler of Europe, being the 'Lord of Navigation, Conquest and Commerce of Ethiopia, Arabia, Persia and India.' Or as the King of France referred to him at the time, 'Lord of the Spices.'

It is no wonder then that armed with the information the Jewish scientists brought with them, the English, the Dutch and the French soon made their way to India via the eastern route and began trading there, despite the Papal decree forbidding it. With the completion of Magellan's voyage, the Spanish could now reach the Orient from the west. The costs of spice started to plummet in Europe. The Portuguese venture in India turned into a heavy financial burden. From that point on, the Portuguese Empire began its gradual and centuries-long decline.

It was then that the distance specified by King João II in the Treaty of Tordesillas, proved of significant importance. With the dividing meridian being 370 leagues west of Africa, Brazil was still in Portuguese territory. Portugal turned to Brazil and began colonizing and trading there in earnest. A governor was appointed in 1549 and slaves were introduced from West Africa to assist in the harvesting of sugar. By 1560 Brazil overtook

Madeira as the chief source of sugar and later on became one of the biggest centers of gold and diamond mines in the world, providing Portugal with great fortunes.

Then came the age of absolutism. The *cortes*, the traditional meeting of the king with the commoners in which grievances were heard, was never summoned again after 1698.

From King João II's time, Portugal gradually fell behind the other European empires. Under Salazar's dictatorship, Portugal still clung onto its colonies by force and was detached from the rest of the world until the bloodless revolution of 1975. The heavy modernization that swept through Europe in the twentieth century had little effect on this small country.

But now with the reins in the hands of the people, Portugal is indeed looking ahead again. And perhaps another Lion, Eagle or a Tiger will come soon.

Chapter 12
COLUMBUS' CONFESSION

My story begins with a birthday. Actually with two birthdays.

The year was 1448. I was born in Portugal and was given the name Salvador Gonçalves Zarco. My mother was Isabel da Câmara, a daughter of the nobleman João Gonçalves Zarco. My father was Dom Fernando, a grandson of King João I of Avis and that made me a descendent of the King. However, my father and mother never married and so at the age of five, she and I moved to the island of Madeira, away from the royal court.

In 1451, a newborn child cried in Italy as he began breathing on his own for the first time. His father, Domenico Colombo, a weaver of woolen cloth in Genoa, took the baby in his arms with joy and thanked the Lord that both his baby and his wife survived the birth. The name of the little boy was Cristoforo Colombo.

At the age of fourteen I moved to Lisbon where I became an apprentice on one of the merchant ships. A few years later, I proudly became a knight of the Order of Christ and having been sworn to absolute secrecy, joined the explorations fleet of Fernão Gomes.

Cristoforo Colombo in the meanwhile, not interested in following his father's business, learned seamanship and sailed around Europe as a merchant.

I learned navigation and piloting in the naval school of Sagres and soon went out on several expeditions, one of which was to the island of Porto Santo where I met a beautiful lady named Filipa. She was the daughter of Bartolomeu Perestrelo, the governor of the island. We fell in love and promised each other that in a few years I would return for her and we would marry.

During the following years I participated in numerous voyages to the West Coast of Africa and working under famed captains and navigators, became proficient in navigation.

Around 1478, the Genoese Colombo settled in Lisbon and acquired a job as a seaman there. Later that year, the ship he was on sank in a storm on its way to the Açores and only the Captain and another man survived. Cristoforo's death was reported with names of the other unfortunates to the governor of São Miguel (an island of the Açores), who was under strict orders to report any sunken ships to Dom João and to him only.

A week later, a man in elegant clothes arrived at Colombo's boarding house in Lisbon. He identified himself as a messenger from the Royal court. He was in search of the home where a seaman named Cristoforo lived. Was that where he lived? The landlady nodded.

The messenger's face lit. Colombo, he explained, had been summoned urgently to Dom João's court and had thus been unable to come and collect his belongings. He had come to take them for Colombo. Of course, this ought to cover any bills he owed, he said handing over a small heavy velvet coin-bag. The landlady gladly showed him to the room.

In the meanwhile I was working aboard Fernão Gomes' ships, exploring the African coast. It was winter of 1478 when I arrived back to my old room at the hostel in Lisbon. There, a royal messenger sent by my cousin Dom João, welcomed me.

"We have been looking for you, *Senhor*," said the messenger, his handsome green jacket with its thin white fur lining hinted at a noble status of some sort. " Dom João is interested in talking with you and sent me to bring you to him."

From the messenger's expression I gathered there was no point in asking questions and quickly put on my best robes. Together we climbed into the inconspicuous covered carriage that waited outside. The horses started off on our way to the Prince's court. Why did my cousin summon me?

As we were passing through the dark woods, the creaking of the carriage wheels and the sound of crushing twigs and leaves under the horses' hooves disturbing the profound silence of the night, I was not able to stop wondering about this secret conference. What was in store for me, the question troubled my mind. Was I in trouble or in favor?

Had I been so careless as to commit breach of confidentiality? If that was true, I would never see the outsides of a prison cell again. I shuddered at the mere thought. My cousin wasn't the type to look the other way even with a relative.

We passed through the castle gate and the sentries, dressed in light mail and carrying lances, closed the heavy doors behind us. The carriage passed across the dimly lit courtyard and stopped by the main house. It was a stately building made of stone, with tall arched windows and wide wooden doors.

We passed through the grand entrance, two guards in brown attire and carrying sizeable swords accompanied us down the narrow hall.

I was led to the Dom João's private quarters and my arrival was announced at the doorway by the guard who was stationed there.

I took a deep breath as I stepped inside the spacious room. Luxury was evident at every corner. The furniture, grand and impressive, was made of special wood, I observed. Carvings of different symbols and designs decorated the sides of the majestic desk and the tall chairs. Thick curtains that carried the Order of Christ emblems covered the shut windows. Two candles shed their flickering illuminations upon the decor befitting a Prince.

Behind the desk sat Dom João, his expression giving away nothing but solemnity. By his side and almost in the shadows, stood Antão de Faria, his chamberlain and right-hand man. The Prince smiled politely in greeting.

He was only twenty-two and had a keen penetrating look that made one feel as though one's soul was being examined.

I bowed slightly in return, unsure what to expect.

"Zarco, my cousin," he began calmly. "You are a knight of the Order of Christ."

A tone of questioning was present in his voice. I nodded to confirm his statement.

"Whether legitimate or not you are a grandson of my grandfather King Duarte, and the royal blood is in your veins just as it is in mine. You are not married and have no close familial ties. You have proven your worth along the coasts of Africa," Dom João then paused for a moment.

"Can I trust you?" he asked suddenly, his glaring eyes searching my face for a reaction.

I maintained my composure. "Of course, my cousin! I will defend you with my body if the need arises. I have observed the rules of secrecy throughout my service to the Order of Christ and torture means nothing to me." And as I was slightly offended I added, "why is it, my good Prince, that you should doubt my loyalty?"

Dom João's stare didn't quiver. Instead he continued to study my expressions and behavior for any clues of my inner feelings. A moment later, as if he had just made up his mind, he spoke again.

"I wouldn't have questioned your fidelity if the matter I was about to discuss with you weren't so delicate and important to our country."

I nodded in understanding.

"You are aware of the threat Spain poses to our gold mines in Africa. Just last week an entire Spanish fleet found its way to the gold coast of Mina and by sheer luck our ships managed to come out victorious. Had the Spanish landed there, they would have seized a considerable amount of gold but more importantly, they would then send more ships there.

"You will agree that this jeopardizes Portugal's claim to Africa and India and at the same time, stirs up a conflict between Portugal and Spain which could result in a war. A war will mean that all discovery voyages and activities will cease and the routes will be open to scavengers who surely will seize the opportunity to take the gold for themselves. Something must be done about it!"

I couldn't agree more. A few years back, my own personal experience of fighting with a pirate Spanish ship off the coast of Africa taught me that they could be greedy and fierce enemies.

"But what can we do?" I asked, unaware of a possible solution. Spain was strong and powerful.

"I have a plan," said the Prince quietly. "A week ago, a Genoese merchant who recently moved to Lisbon, died tragically on a voyage to the Açores. Portugal will owe him a lot for his service, for even though he is not with us anymore, his identity shall remain live."

I frowned in bewilderment.

"You, my friend, shall take on his identity," carried on the Prince. "From now on your name will be Cristoforo Colombo, or Cristovão Colom in Portuguese. You will use this name and this name alone. Here are his books, notes and personal correspondence. In the improbable case that a message arrives from his family in Italy, respond to it as if he were alive.

"I will arrange for you to marry the woman of your choice regardless of your new commoner status. When the right opportunity arrives, you will move to Spain and distract the Spanish from the African route."

The Prince went on to describe his plot as I listened. Obviously, I had a lot to sacrifice. But on the other hand, here was a chance to serve my country like no other man had done in the past. I was a knight of the Order of Christ and to serve the King of Portugal was an honor. I wasn't the same man when I left the court that night.

I returned to Lisbon and acquired a room under my new name. I found a new job aboard a ship that headed to the far and frozen lands of the north and sailed the powerful North Atlantic Sea. That same year, I visited Iceland and Greenland where the fish were plenty and the cod was in abundance. We soon returned to Lisbon and Dom João called for me again. This time we discussed whom I should marry. We agreed that Filipa Perestrelo, the young lady I had met in Porto Santo was a good choice. I loved her and she was of a good family.

After some questioning on the island of Porto Santo, I found out that Filipa had joined a convent in Portugal and didn't want to get married. We had given each other a promise. How could she break it? I was determined to find her and at least talk to her.

A few weeks later I showed up at the convent's doorstep demanding to see Filipa. At first, the head nun wouldn't permit it, but after many persuasive maneuvers, I managed to convince her to let me in. My heart skipped a beat when I saw Filipa standing there in the garden, a white garment covering her beautiful figure.

And right there, in front of the head nun and the others, I begged her to fulfil her old promise to me. With tears of joy in her eyes, she agreed and we went off to get married. The head nun's reaction is better off censored.

Though she never inquired as to why I had changed my name, I had told her before our marriage that I had a life-long mission to accomplish as a knight of the Order of Christ which required that I assume a different identity. She accepted it and promised that she would follow me in my quest without asking questions.

I was very happy with my new life. Dom João sent for me whenever he needed a service and paid generously. A year later, Filipa gave birth to my son, Diogo. I in turn joined the center of discoveries in Sagres and sailed to Africa and to Madeira while keeping myself abreast of any new maps and navigational developments.

In 1481, Dom João, became King João II. But even with his new title he never forgot his cousin. He supplied me, always through messengers, with ample support.

The gold and riches brought back from Africa strengthened the Portuguese Crown and with the King's reforms, the country was in a state of great tension. The nobles were dissatisfied with the King's new policies and growing power and felt his existence endangered theirs while the commoners and merchants rejoiced in their newfound protector.

In 1483 the Duke of Bragança was found guilty of conspiracy against the King and was executed, thus effectively removing the only firm Portuguese ally Spain had in the country. Portugal's influence and power was increasing rapidly and Queen Isabel and King Fernando were becoming concerned.

In 1484, a royal messenger contacted me discreetly and after ensuring we weren't followed, led me to the royal stable where in the dark, I met with the King alone. A few years had passed since we had last met in person and his features seemed more sage and learned, but his keen penetrating glare was still very much the same.

"The time has come, hasn't it?" I asked, sensing his discomfort.

The King nodded reluctantly.

"My cousin, it is with great honor that I shall carry out my assignment. You mustn't feel guilty for sending me to Spain," I encouraged him. It seemed to cheer him up slightly.

"You are a brave man, Salvador Zarco," He said. The mention of my long-forgotten name echoed through my head as if my deepest of secrets had just been discovered. "I and the entire kingdom will never forget your loyalty and dedication." For a second, I could have sworn I saw his eyes turn slightly misty. It was dark in the stable and whether I had indeed seen his tear or not, I have always liked to believe that I had. King João was a man of magnificent self-control but at the same time was full of compassion.

"After tonight," he said, "we will have to be very wise and careful. One mistake could risk our route to India or even cost you your life. You must pay close attention to what I am about to tell you.

"In three months' time, you will come to me with a proposal to head a discovery voyage. Your objective will be to reach India from the west. This theory was presented to me by an Italian named Toscanelli some time ago and you should become familiar with it as if you had been studying it for years. I will reject your proposal and you will move to Spain, frustrated that you were unable to obtain my cooperation.

"In Spain you will present yourself to the Queen and King of Spain as a Genoese, trained in navigation by the Portuguese and lay your theory before them. Your goal is to convince them of the feasibility of this plan and to finance your westward voyage to India."

The King stopped for a moment and unfolded a map. I let out a quiet sigh, thinking about the risk involved. I had to be strong, I told myself. He carried on.

"Once they agree, you will travel to the West, remaining the entire time south of the Canary Islands. You will reach the Indies," he pointed to a group of islands on the map that was along the same latitude as Cape Verde. "You must study this map with great thoroughness and once able to remember the location of these islands, destroy it." He handed the map over.

The map was no ordinary map, I observed. It was a map of the known world and had a rough outline of a long continent stretching from pole to pole on the other side of the Atlantic. At the bottom of the map were advanced charts and tables that I had never seen before. I tucked it in my deepest pocket.

"Once you return, I will summon you to my court and you must be as brash as you can in light of your discovery. Try to keep the Spanish interested in the west as long as you sensibly can. If you ever receive a letter from me apologizing for having ignored your proposal, it will be a warning that an enemy knows about your true identity and that you should escape across the border back to Portugal.

"I may make attempts to persuade you to return to Portugal or even send people to sabotage your journey, in order to make the Spanish believe more firmly in your westward journeys. However, I will never apologize formally in a letter or by a messenger unless the circumstances are truly dangerous. Is there anything I have overlooked?"

"No, my King. The plan is without a flaw," I responded earnestly.

King João II looked square in my eyes for a full minute and finally wished God to be with me. He turned around and walked out.

I stood there for a while, contemplating my position. The future of Portugal rested on my shoulders. However, I was a grandson of a king and was born prepared for such responsibilities.

I often discreetly studied the map and charts the King

had given me till I was able to visualize them in my head in complete detail. I read Toscanelli's essays, Marco Polo's writings and other works by honorable people such as Pope Pius II and Pierre d'Ailly. Toscanelli's interpretation of Marco Polo's writing indicated China and the island of Japan were close to the west of Europe. But I knew from my experience that any self-respecting navigator in the Portuguese court would have known this to be impossible.

Additionally, did Marco Polo ever sail the Atlantic Ocean? Did Toscanelli ever attempt to discover India for himself? No, they did not. To me it seemed like the Italians were attempting to intentionally misdirect Portugal's efforts to the west. Their spice trade with the Muslims brought them great riches. Surely their near-monopoly would disappear should Portugal reach India by sea!

My King was too smart to be thrown off by Toscanelli's ideas, but figured out how to use these, with a little help from Colombo, to misdirect his enemies. Years ago I saw the land to the west with my own eyes. Its coasts were wild and unpopulated and its seas gave no clue of the great trade and commerce of the Orient. It was not India.

But in order to develop an enthusiastic attitude toward my plan, I felt I had to encourage the curiosity within me and guide it toward the west in some way. And one evening, stooped over maps dimly lit with candlelight, I found the way. If it was not India, what was this land? The nameless golden beaches and the uncharted coasts fascinated my attention. A new land was ahead and I was destined to explore it.

Instinctively, I had shared my newly developed plan with Filipa, explaining Toscanelli's theory to her in great detail. She loved listening and was an excellent audience. But my Filipa was also a curious woman. She would ask questions and pose arguments in an attempt to disprove the theory, and I would reply in its defense. Thus, our late night "arguments" were the perfect practice for my presentation to the King. Soon I found that the desire to head an expedition into the unknown was truly growing roots in my heart. Why not explore the land beyond the Atlantic?

And so, in late 1484, I presented my theory to the King and his advisors with such great eloquence and confidence that even the King raised an eyebrow at my zeal. My performance became more than an act and I spoke what I really felt inside. But I made sure I looked straight into my King's eyes and that was all I needed to do to rest his mind to rest. He and only he could tell that I was still following his orders.

King João II dismissed my plan with the excuse that none of his advisors saw any possibility of success in my venture, but not without a discreet smile denoting his pleasure at my well-executed part.

I returned home in low spirits. My plan was turned down but I was prepared for that. The move to Spain was not as easy to adjust to.

I told Filipa what had happened and she consoled me with great sympathy. There are other ways and means of achieving your dream, she whispered softly. She expressed her confidence in me and said she thought my theory was correct. It was her way of telling me to do what I had to do.

A few weeks later I informed Filipa of my intentions to move to Spain and attempt to convince the Spanish monarchs to support my plan. Her first reaction was anger. Why Spain? Didn't I see what would happen if Spain got to India before Portugal? I begged her to not question my loyalty to my country.

She was no fool and after intense meditation she had formed her own idea about my mission. Oh, how I wanted to explain everything to her. But that would betray my King. She eventually conceded and said she would keep her promise to follow me wherever I went. The relief I felt was surprising. I hadn't realized how much I needed her. That night we held on to each other in a way we never had before.

The following weeks were spent in preparation for our move to Spain. Many things had to be taken care of.

I was in high-spirits, feeling the Lord was on my side. So far everything went according to plan. Little did I know how soon the gray doom clouds would hang over my head.

One evening I returned home to find a nurse at the house. Filipa was in bed in high fever. She had caught the plague! My kind neighbor offered me a room temporarily. I was prohibited from seeing Filipa while she was ill. And it wasn't long before the hopes of her recovery were shattered and I found myself kissing her hand as she took her last breath.

I was devastated by her death and the following days passed by in sordid desperation. Living without Filipa seemed impossible. The only thing that kept me alive was my promise to the King. I had to carry on, I told myself repeatedly. In her memory, I swore to never shave my beard again and to this day I have followed my vow.

The anonymous letter that arrived with words of consolation was in the King's personal handwriting, and that helped me somewhat to recover. It was nearly 1485 before I finally regained enough courage and determination to make my way to Spain.

Leaving my young son in the care of Filipa's sister, my journey to Spain was relatively easy as I was alone.

My services were accepted at one of the noble houses in Spain, where I assisted in different ways the management of the house, all the time promoting my interest in the western voyage to India and Cipango.

I became acquainted with a nobleman from Seville who shared my views about the west and using his name made it possible for me to lay my plan before the Crown of Spain.

I was ushered into the spacious hall in their great palace where the King and Queen sat on their impressive thrones. The splendid decorations and impressive furniture gave the room an aura of richness and grandeur, while the bare stone walls and the simple curtains added a touch of practicality, a characteristic not lacking in the two rulers. Beside the powerful Spanish rulers stood their most trusted advisor and behind the three were two heavily armed royal guards.

I talked for an hour perhaps, explaining my theory using the best of my persuasive skills. Keeping my mind focused on the fact that there was land across the Atlantic, India or otherwise, I was able to relay it with such conviction that I even surprised myself.

The Rulers of Castile expressed their doubts about the accuracy of my plans, but in light of my five years of experience under Portuguese captains and navigators, did not dismiss me at once. They asked their advisor to research my plan in detail and propose his recommendations once that was done. With the help of my noble ally from Seville, I had managed to convince the advisor to the Crown of the merits of my plan and he promised he would do his best to assist me once the crusade in the south was over.

The Spanish began their crusade against the remaining Muslims in the south of Spain some time before and were occupied with the war for several years. The Portuguese, temporarily undisturbed by Spanish poachers, continued their explorations vigorously, and in December 1488, Bartolomeu Dias rounded the African Cape of Good Hope under King João's flag.

King João summoned me to his court again under the pretext that he desired me to submit my plans to him again. But in actual fact, it was designed to receive information on my progress. Due to the presence of his advisors and guards, I mentioned to him casually of what I had been doing since our last conference and hinted at the fact that the Spanish were showing interest in my plan. The King then pretended to become occupied with Dias' recent discovery of Cape of Good Hope and dismissed me again. I could see from his expression that he was satisfied with my accomplishments so far.

With the successful conquest of Granada from the Muslims came the opportunity of addressing the King and Queen again. Their advisor favored my proposal as he had promised and the Crown, anxious to catch up with Portugal and ready to invest in maritime explorations, agreed to finance my venture.

In August 1492, the moment I had been waiting for arrived.

The three ships under my command were ready to sail off to the west.

The departure ceremony was grand and joyous. The King and Queen arrived with their court, the royal family and the nobles. Several Church leaders attended and gave their blessings. Sailors gave a last kiss to their wives before the voyage. Young apprentices said goodbye to their parents. The port was crowded with commoners and merchants alike and the excitement was inspiring.

Soon, I told myself as the massive ships started on their way, we will be sailing into the unknown, coasting along unexplored territory and expanding the Faith to the numerous heathens who inhabit it.

The rest is covered in my diary in great detail. On October 12th, 1492, one of the sailors pointed out land. My voyage was considered a success back in Spain and I headed three additional voyages during the following decade. News reached my ears that in the meantime Vasco de Gama of Portugal had reached India by sea. I had accomplished the mission my King had entrusted me with.

Having successfully side-tracked Spain to the west, securing Portugal's undisturbed route to India, I retired to Valladolid.

And now, I am bed-ridden and my days are numbered. I have written my story and have entrusted it to my confessor to keep. Knowing that I had carried out my King's will and have given unselfish service to my country, Portugal, I am now prepared to depart.

(Author's note:

The document that I consider most conclusive in proving that America's discovery was not as straightforward as history claims, is in fact a record of Columbus' own words.

In 1498, when he set sail on his third voyage, which took him for the first time to the coast of South America, he stated that he intended to find out what King João II had meant by saying that there was a continent to the southwest of the Atlantic. The date or circumstances around the King's utterance is not known.

However, how could King João possibly be aware of such a continent if it wasn't yet "discovered"?

The easiest route to Africa was to sweep a wide circle

southwest nearly touching the South American coast, and then at the appropriate latitude sail east and round the Cape of Good Hope. The easiest return route was to sail north along the African Coast, around Guinea sweep another wide circle westward using the semi-permanent westbound winds of the tropics and return via the Azores on the wings of the eastbound Westerlies. In both cases, they sometimes had sailed much further west in the process.

Constantly repeated tales were told of the land far west. A coast dimly seen through the clouds, a scent of land carried by the wind, floating weeds and the flight of birds were the occasional odd sights and experiences that indicated a landmass or a large group of islands existed to the west. But nothing of the tales suggested any of the busy seas and ports of India or Japan described by Marco Polo.

In January 1474, a great seaman, João Vaz Corte-Real sailed under Dom João's instructions far up north into the regions of the frozen seas. Where he went and what he found is not recorded, but it is known he was rewarded by the Dom João for discovering the "Land of Codfish," possibly Newfoundland.

In 1486 there is evidence in maps of westward voyages from the Azores in quest of the semi-legendary islands St. Brendan, Antillia and Brazil. These are explained to have been chartmakers' reduplication of the known Atlantic Islands, but this is not a settled matter.

In 1514, a letter to the King of Portugal was received from a Portuguese merchant taken prisoner on Spanish territory north of Brazil. It tells how he had been shipwrecked and thrown into jail despite the fact that he was on his way to another coast east of the dividing line – a country "visited by Your Highness' subjects and known to them for over twenty years."

Another document of 1531 that tells of a Brazilian fort in Pernambuco (known as Recife these days) says that this site had been "inhabited by Portuguese who had been living there upwards of forty years." That would have placed its colonization at latest 1491!

The chronicle by the Spanish historian Las Casas mentions that the natives of Antilles told Columbus upon his arrival that they had seen other white and bearded men some years before!

And then the most incredible fact lies with the famous Treaty of Tordesillas. King João intentionally moved the proposed dividing meridian from 100 leagues off Cape Verde Islands to 370 leagues. Neither 200 leagues nor 300 leagues, but specifically 370 leagues. This change proved later on to secure Brazil as Portuguese territories and if one cut the world in half at the said meridian, on the Orient side of the world the Spanish half would include Japan but not India!

What was the reason behind King João's decision to move the meridian to that exact distance is to this date not documented. It wasn't to protect Africa, as the first proposed meridian left Portugal with total control over the Africa coast and the Indian Ocean. The only sensible conclusion is that King João II knew exactly what he was doing when he signed the Treaty of Tordesillas whereas the Spanish rulers did not.

Although no "concrete" evidence had been found to prove it, the letters and facts I have mentioned are, in my opinion, proof of Portugal's secret knowledge and colonization of South America as early as 1491, three years prior to Columbus' discovery of the South American Coast.

Perhaps no "concrete" documents exist because King João II kept his activities and plans secret to such a degree that even to this date, no modern historian is sure as to the extent of his knowledge.

Columbus was educated in cartography and navigation in Portugal where the world's best scientists congregated at that time. Is it not strange that he would overlook their opinions and calculations so obstinately, being a navigator with an avid interest in cartography and astronomy?

Upon Columbus' return from his first voyage, he made a stop in Portugal first (supposedly due to a storm) and was summoned by King João II again. The King's chronicler describes their conversation as an outrage. Columbus was rather above himself and described the land he discovered, its fabulous beaches, the vegetation and its abundance of fruit and flowers, indirectly pointing out the King's mistake for refusing to support him earlier.

The King listened with dismay, perhaps intentionally, giving Columbus the pleasure of seeing him appear regretful. The King's men were ready to apprehend the man and whispered in the King's ear a plan to rid of Columbus and his tales, which were an embarrassment to the Portuguese Crown. The King solemnly forbade them to do that and dismissed Columbus with a handsome gift. Under no circumstance should Columbus, his men or ships be harmed, ordered the King. Why had King João II tolerated Columbus' rudeness, protected him and presented him with a gift?

These loose ends intrigued me.

After some research, I have concluded there are only three options that would reconcile the mystery:

1) Columbus was indeed Genoese and was not in King João's service. In this case one must admit that given all the above facts, Columbus must have been a fool to ignore the facts and figures which the best navigators in the world proved were incorrect. Supposedly till his last day he believed that he had indeed reached India.

2) Columbus was just after his own fame. He knew that across the Atlantic was not India but just another undiscovered land and simply desired the personal glory using the Spanish's resources.

3) King João already had an intricate spy network in and out of Portugal. Why shouldn't he take advantage of Toscanelli's theory of the west route to India and send one of his men to Spain to misdirect them?

A Portuguese couldn't be sent there, as he would immediately be suspect and to send a foreigner as a spy was out of the question: loyalty was a very rare and precious commodity in those days.

The King had to send a loyal Portuguese under

disguise. Columbus was Genoese in origin and was in Portugal for six years in total, some of which were spent aboard discovery ships. What could have been a better cover for his spy who was actually a cousin of royal blood whom he could trust with the task?

Surely North America held nothing for him or for Portugal which was of value at the time. Gold wasn't on the surface as it was in the Gold Coast, spice wasn't available as it was in India and no opportunities of fighting the Muslim existed there. The only thing it offered was the codfish, which evidently was being fished there by the Portuguese anyway.

Brazil on the other hand, offered ports where the merchants going to India could rest. It additionally gave Portugal the command of the South Atlantic, as Africa and Brazil lay relatively close to each other along the seaway. Perhaps João II also knew South America held riches that only a later generation would have the resources to explore.

If Columbus was indeed King João's secret agent, he surely deserves more appreciation for his spying talents than for his navigational abilities. To have fooled the rulers of Castile for an entire decade would have required some considerable skill.

In any event, King João got his way. While the Spanish were sailing around the Antilles, Brazil was secured as a Portuguese territory and Portugal was the first to reach India via the eastern route.)

Chapter 13
"NUN BELLIES" OR "ANGEL TITS"?

I find real traditional Portuguese desserts to be quite mysterious. They aren't common in restaurants and aren't usually sold in *pastelarias*.

Fortunately, I had the privilege of being invited to meet a group of experts on the subject in order to answer some of the burning questions that I had on my mind. It was scheduled to take place on a Sunday evening in a small house in Oeiras, near Lisbon.

About seven o'clock, I climbed the old stairs which were covered with thick carpet, the aged wood creaking under the weight of my steps.

On the second floor was the apartment of the elderly hostess, *Dona* Gina. I knocked and the door opened a crack. Her face appeared and with a welcoming smile she opened the door wide and urged me to come in.

Inside, the tasteful furniture was especially arranged for the occasion. Several antique padded chairs with wooden legs and backs, were placed around the living room opposite the large and comfortable sofa. A few recipe and Portuguese cuisine books sat upon the fireplace mantel.

Around the long knee-high rectangular coffee table sat the rest of the "council" members: Gina's brother Manuel António and his wife Maria Luisa as well as Gina's other brother Luis and his wife Ivone. Gina and Maria Luisa were knowledgeable in the Alentejo specialties while Ivone was the authority on the Algarve ones. They were all grandparents but looked quite young for their age.

After handshakes and *beijinhos*, I sat down. They noisily chatted away while I was gathering my notes. The way they were talking so energetically made it seem like I was attending an evening with teenagers rather than elders. Throughout the conference, smaller conversations continued between those not directly involved in answering my questions.

As soon as I was ready, Gina looked at me expectantly.

"What exactly are the *doces conventuais*?" my first question officially opened the Q & A session.

"The story begins in the eleventh century at the time of the conquest of Portugal from the Moors," she started and let out a deep sigh, as if beginning a lecture. "The King set up convents and monasteries as a way to populate and take ownership of any newly conquered land as well as making his presence felt by the infidel.

"Several customs kept the convents full. A daughter who was not married by a certain age would be sent by her family to join the convent. Ladies in trouble were often sent there as well. Those who were inclined toward religion also joined."

It seemed to me that if society followed these rules today, the world would become one large convent with millions of nuns. But I kept my opinions to myself.

"When the ladies of well-to-do families joined the convent," she continued, "they usually brought a large dowry with them as if they were getting married. The convent in turn promised to care for them for life. It thus became an easy venture to start a convent. By the fourteenth and fifteenth centuries, the number of convents was so high that official Bulls decreed that no more convents were to be established in Portugal!"

"The convents served as safe lodgings for the King and his court," started Maria Luisa, "while he traveled around the country. For various reasons, they sought to please the King during his stays as well as gain the support of the local nobles.

"Those convents which treated the King and nobles superbly, got special attention in return. Choosing the convent as a burial site, bestowing monies on the convent in one's will and constructing a new chapel were all actions these men of power could take to show their gratitude. All of this meant good income for the convent, which had to maintain itself and its members --"

Ivone interrupted, getting to the point. "In order to strike the King's and noblemen's fancy, the convents would put on the best celebrations possible in their honor. Part of the festivities was to serve special delicious desserts for them. The nuns were thus often occupied not with prayer but with creating outstanding sweet dishes. Nuns who came from wealthy families often brought their own recipes of various sweets and pastries with them. To be known as the best host became a group endeavor in each convent."

"Those desserts which were created in the convents," Gina gained control of the discussion again, "are known as *doces conventuais* and *doces de ovos*. Many of these were given rather 'holy' names, some of which were rather strange."

"Such as what?"

"*Barrigas de freira*, for example," she suggested. "This is a cake made of a fluffy mixture of egg yolks and sugar, shaped like a loaf of bread. The servings are cut much like bread slices and are usually topped with sweet syrup."

"Or *papos de anjo*." Ivone added. "These look like sweet muffins but with flat tops and are also made of cooked egg yolks and served with a sugar syrup."

"And *toucinho do céu*," added Maria Luisa. *Toucinho do céu* means 'heaven's bacon' -- obviously not a name originated by the Jews. "Heaven's bacon is a round cake made of a mixture of almond paste, eggs and sugar," she explained.

By now the men, who up to that point were involved in another discussion, could not restrain themselves from interrupting. From their enthusiasm, I concluded that they were avid dessert consumers.

"What about *fios de ovos*?" cried Manuel António.

"And what about *trouxas de ovos*?" asked Luis, amazed that his favorite dessert had gone unmentioned.

They went on to argue about which was the best confection while I attempted to catch up on my notes. A few questions arose in my mind. First, the indecent names. How did they arrive at 'bellies' and 'tities'? And not only that but in a convent?

Secondly, this egg business seemed odd. Why are there so many sweets made of eggs? For me, eggs are usually scrambled, "sunny-side-upped" or "omeletted," accompanied by a side dish of hash browns, French fries or grits; not an ingredient put into a dessert.

But I didn't want to put them in a spot with such tactless questions. These questions belonged to library research.

A few days later, I learned from an informative book about Portuguese cuisine, that following the great number of convents that were established in the thirteenth and fourteenth centuries, discreet relationships between nuns, monks and members of the aristocracy became a growing occurrence. It grew to such a degree that in the eighteenth centuries explicit orders were issued to curb such behavior! No wonder then, that names like 'nun bellies' and 'angel tits' sprouted in the convents.

The only logical explanation I could arrive at for the egg sweets was that Portugal was the primary provider of sugar in Europe around the fifteenth century. The easiest way to purify sugar is by pouring egg whites over the sugar. The dust and impurities are swept away by the egg whites and one is left with pure sugar and lots of egg yolks. It couldn't have been too long before someone mixed the two, cooked it and found it to be savory.

By now, everybody was intently conversing about interesting places to visit in the Alentejo and it appeared they had forgotten about the desserts. I was ready to fire away with the next question and eventually managed to catch Gina's attention.

"*Dona* Gina, why can't I usually find these desserts in restaurants?" I asked.

"Well," she whispered, looking secretive. "These desserts are passed on from generation to generation and many families have their own secret ways of preparing them which they don't share with others.

"Even if one gets the recipe, one must watch how it is done as the correct way of cooking these desserts can only be learned from actual observation and practice. No recipe could ever describe exactly how to cook them. If a recipe says to cook the sugar until its drops look like pearls, how could anyone know exactly what it means? One has to see it to understand what is meant by pearls. It's a matter of an acquired skill."

"When I was thirteen," Maria Luisa joined in, "my mother taught me how to cook my first egg-type dessert. It's called "black woman's kiss" which is the easiest one to make. Then I gradually learned to prepare the others."

"She does great *papos de anjo*!" exclaimed Manuel António, licking his lips at the thought.

"But the fact is that the number of people who know how to prepare them is much smaller these days. Those few who are skilled at cooking them usually make them for the family, for special occasions or for sale to restaurants," said Gina. "This is why they are hard to find."

That made sense. I have gone from restaurant to restaurant in Cascais and it is true, they are not common. Also, not many foreigners know about them (and if they do they treat these egg desserts with utmost suspicion) and so restaurants tend to offer more common desserts.

What a shame, I thought. This tradition had been kept in existence solely through older generations teaching the younger ones, and is slowly being lost.

I was shown the special tools used in cooking the egg desserts. There were different sizes of golden pots made of an alloy of copper and tin, the only alloy that allows eggs to retain their bright yellow color while being cooked. There was a strange small pitcher with two thin and long spouts which was used to make long strands of eggs, a technique used in some of the more fancy egg desserts.

Encouraged by the men, the conversation soon became a discussion about other desserts such as almonds and marzipan and even began to touch upon some delicious main dishes. One of Gina's young relatives came, bringing along a present. It was an eel that her brother had fished only two hours before. "It is so fresh it is almost still alive," she warned.

Gradually, the meeting turned into a relaxed family gathering.

A bit later, all got up to leave and I made sure I

thanked each one of them for their considerate help and valuable information. A ceremony of handshaking and *bejinhos* followed and soon everyone went their way.

I was pondering how fortunate I was to get the skinny on the egg desserts. However, I realized that if I was to write about them, I had to experience these sweet confections first-hand. There was no escape. Duty called and I was destined to go on a dessert-tasting tour (poor me.) Oh well, a writer can't write without research...

The following morning, I awoke as the bright sun was slowly peeping above the horizon. I collected my things and set on my journey. My eyelids were heavier than cast iron anvils and so I allowed my little Fiat to lead me along the road.

It must have done a good job as I can't quite remember how I got to the local *pastelaria*.

This particular *pastelaria* was a large one. The scents of fresh bread and pastry filled my nose even before I stepped in. Through the sizeable glass display case which exhibited an overwhelming number of cookies and cakes, I stared at the numerous different types of temptations like a kid does in a candy store (I managed to resist pressing my face against the glass though.)

First there were several kinds of French pastry (*palmiers*, *éclairs*, etc.) which are baked daily in all *pastelarias*.

Then there were the *pasteis*. These cup-like pastries with sweet concoctions inside were prepared with all sorts of fruity ingredients. *Pastel de côco* was made of coconut while *pastel de laranja* was definitely orange. *Pastel de feijão* was an odd one since it was made of beans, but tasted surprisingly delicious.

As I was looking over to find out what was next, a man in a white apron came holding a wide baking pan full of cookies. Their fresh aroma filled the room quickly and their vapor trail proved they were still hot. He laid the pan on the aluminum shelf behind the display counter and transferred them into their appropriate trays.

The huge selection of cookies ranged from flat biscuit-like pastries to round balls of chocolate and included the different heavenly almond confections. I seriously considered hiding somewhere until closing time arrived and everybody had left, and then just have a feast.

I soon gave up trying to list all these mouth-watering sights, as no descriptions could relay their appetizing appearance, and concluded that I could only recommend to the reader to go to a large *pastelaria* and experience them for himself.

I eventually ordered a *bica* and *a pão de Deus,* 'the bread of God'. I waited to find out what it was in anticipation. The bread of God must be something special, I thought, expecting a large heavy cake. After a minute, a small plate arrived with the awaited pastry on a napkin in its center. The medium sized sweet bun was thick and fat, and its top layer was sprinkled with coconut. My dream of a giant cake vanished in an instant. I finally took a bite. It was a simple pastry, but its taste was heavenly.

A while later, as I was trailing along the northeast-bound roads, the rural scenery replaced the multilevel apartment buildings, factories and commercial centers. A unique type of wilderness exists in this region, the Ribatejo, which is in one way similar to and in another way different from that of the Alentejo. The greenery is composed mostly of olive and eucalyptus trees. Occasional cork oaks show their true colors with their exposed reddish trunks. Pine forests are also present here and there.

Driving down the long and winding country road, it appeared that the Little Man from the Signage Department had done an excellent job in preventing his colleagues from placing road-signs at every corner, and I thanked him once again for preserving nature. I even entertained the thought of sharing a bottle of wine with him one day.

But then, of course, I got lost as there were no signs whatsoever to point the way and I dismissed the idea with a snarl. After seeking directions on numerous occasions, which were always repeated several times by the friendly people along the way, I managed to get back on the right track. By now it was lunch time and I stopped at the *Caravela*, a roadside restaurant in Santo Estêvão, a small village near Coruche.

The cordial owner served me himself -- he was the only one there -- while his wife cooked in the kitchen. He spoke very good English and told me about his past employment aboard large cruise ships. He had been all over the world, but now needed to rest a bit and therefore had moved here for some peace and quiet.

I ordered the recommended dish, *feijoada de peixe,* a stew of seafood and beans. The owner warned me against eating the appetizers, as the dish demanded a healthy appetite. Foolishly I disregarded his advice and had a few sneak bites. The entrée arrived in a gigantic pot. I stared at it for a full minute. If any of the dishes were large in previous chapters, this one outdid them by far. It could have sustained an army of soldiers for a month.

But it was delicious beyond words. Large prawns, small shrimps, tiny sea muscles and slices of squid were mixed in with the beans. The taste was outstanding and the white Alentejo wine complemented it nicely. At the end of the meal, the pot was still half full.

I rested for some time before I managed to muster enough strength to ask for details on their desserts. They had a *toucinho do céu* and a *doce de amêndoa*, a special almond confection which I was urged to try. Since it was a trip dedicated to dessert examination, I ordered both without any remorse of conscience.

The *toucinho do céu* proved to live up to its reputation and had an exquisite taste. I could sense the abounding egg yolks but they were sweet, and I readily agreed that with the marzipan added in, it was an excellent dessert.

The almond dish appeared shortly after in a glass dessert bowl. It was superb, light and sweet, with a distinct nutty flavor. I finished it cheerfully, knowing that my sins were well justified.

I lingered as usual over a *carioca de limão* and having

thanked the owner for the excellent meal, "rolled" to my car.

Shortly after, I had to pull over in Ponte de Sor. A small sign announced that a local café/restaurant named *A Cenoura,* ('the carrot') featured Portuguese specialty desserts. I asked a passerby for directions and watched in amazement as he started walking and motioned me to follow him. Striding around the corner with me driving slowly behind him, he led me to it. I thanked him profusely for his kindness and he accepted my gratitude with a large smile.

Inside, only one table was still occupied as lunch was already over. Six men were sitting and chatting there, and I counted six empty bottles of wine as well as an empty bottle of whisky. At the moment they were at the *café* stage of the meal.

Of the five traditional desserts on display, I chose the one that seemed most appealing. The *sericaia,* an egg dessert, was a thin, golden-brown cake that looked like a tart. By itself it was tasty though not very sweet, but several candied plums in thick syrup added on the side sweetened it beautifully. I was informed that it was possibly brought over from India but certainly was very popular in the Vila Viçosa Palace. I envied the Portuguese Kings and lords of those days.

Due to physical reasons, I was unable to try any others and returned to my car. As I was motoring along the rural roads, I suddenly arrived at an ancient bridge. The road across, made of large cobblestone with tall stone edges was supported by a series of arches. The small inconspicuous sign at the other end announced that the *ponte da Vila Formosa* was a Roman bridge dating back to the second century. And here it was in perfect condition, still in use today. The Romans really built things to last.

I skipped dinner but navigated to another restaurant known for its traditional dessert near Abrantes. There I had yet another, and even more intriguing dessert.

It was my first encounter with *baba de camelo*. I learned the meaning of its name, "camel's drool," only after I had ordered it, and as the waiter was placing it in front of me I realized there was no escape. I would have to consume the camel's drool.

What sort of an appetizing name is that anyway? I thought to myself as I inspected what was inside the small glass bowl. It was a slightly foam-flecked mousse-like concoction, with a light beige color. With some hesitation, I collected a bit on my spoon and tasted it. I was amazed at its savory and smooth characteristics. Made out of condensed milk, eggs and crumbled biscuits, it was thicker and denser than a regular mousse in composition but its taste was rather light.

As I was scooping the last few drops of *baba de camelo* off the bottom of the bowl, I reflected at how these nuns really knew their business. Having indulged myself to the limit, I resignedly admitted my research was now complete. I thanked the Lord for creating so many convents in Portugal, without which all of these excellent desserts wouldn't exist.

Like all sweets, ice cream is very popular in Portugal and it would be a crime not to mention it in this chapter.

During the hot months of summer, hundreds of thousands of ice cream bars, cones and bowls are put to the test of how fast these chilly magic wands can cool down one's body and soul. It seems that the majority of them passes, evidenced by the increasing number of *Olá* and *Camy* ice cream posters which are on display outside restaurants and kiosks.

On a very hot day, a specific billboard which advertises ice cream illustrates one's feelings rather accurately. It shows a man biting on a frozen ice cream bar, his eyes are open wide with relief and his hair is covered with frost. Whenever I see this poster, I cannot agree more and I buy one to cool me down. It works every time.

But, if you want to have a unique ice cream, I will let the cat out of the bag.

Located in the center of Cascais next to the main walking street, is an old-fashioned ice-cream house that is out of this world. Its name is *Santini*.

Its entrance is small and not covered by neon signs, but inside it is designed like any establishment that sells excellent ice cream should be. Close by the entrance is the cashier where you order and pay. Then, behind a wide and long white counter, stand several servers in white aprons ready to prepare the ice cream cone of your dreams.

All right, so you might not be a little kid and licking ice cream from a cone may no longer be your favorite late evening snack. But perhaps if you try it, you will feel young again for a while, depending on how many scoops you get. So I heartily recommend it. This does not mean, of course, that if one wants to stay young, one should eternally eat ice cream, although it sounds like an interesting idea...

The walls all around are covered by mirrors with colorful abstract sketches imprinted upon them. Small tables with glass tops and white, round-backed chairs are positioned along the wall. At the far end, there are two booths where larger groups can sit.

As I paid for my order, I noticed an unusual smell in the air. I took in a few short breaths in an attempt to identify what it was. The friendly cashier (who was the owner) dispelled the mystery for me.

"What you are smelling is the aroma of home-made ice cream," he explained and smiled.

"Oh?" I asked with raised eyebrows. Yeah, another "a hundred percent natural preservatives and coloring ice cream." I know the trick.

After looking over the shop and seeing there were no immediate clients to take care of, he led me to the kitchen.

There he showed me boxes upon boxes of fresh fruit. Strawberries, melons, bananas, berries and others were all there in their places. It smelled as though I was in the middle of a field full of trees bearing ripe fruit.

Even the vanilla, usually made out of extract aided by chemicals, was made with the real thing. He pulled a plastic bag out of the fridge and opened it up. A strong aroma of vanilla filled the air about us as he pulled out a short thin bean, resembling licorice candy. This is the fruit of the vanilla climbing orchids, and its price is ten-fold that of synthetic vanilla.

The fruit are inspected, rinsed and then put into a special juicer machine, he explained. Every morning tens of kilos of each fruit was made into juice for the fresh ice cream. The juice would be mixed in with cream and sugar, blended and put into the freezer. A few hours later, the ice creams were ready. *Santini* was truly a natural ice cream, no doubt about it.

Impressed with the way they prepared it and ready to have a taste, I returned to the main room.

There were many flavors to choose from and it took me a while to decide. I took so long that the man serving me even started tapping his fingers absentmindedly while waiting. Eventually I selected three flavors and the cone full of ice cream was immediately presented to me with a smile.

I tasted it and it was outstanding. I could really feel the fruit in the ice cream; it was incredible. It couldn't be compared to regular ice creams. The melon flavor was especially superb and tasted just like the fruit itself.

I left full of ice cream but very satisfied.

Coming to Portugal, one definitely is better off leaving all diets behind, as this country is a never-ending source for wonderful, tasty cakes, pastries and desserts. And these are so well appreciated by the people that they have even become part of the Portuguese tradition.

My final question is that if one wanted to truly experience Portugal, wouldn't one have to try each of the hundreds of traditional types of sweets? I think you know the answer.

Chapter 14
THE MEANING OF LIFE

A recent Portuguese song put things into perspective.

The song is about how wonderful life is. It details a man's feelings as he wakes up in the morning with his loved one by his side and then goes out to drink a coffee.

At first I thought it a humorous exaggeration, but soon learned the song was indeed true. Life in Portugal proved to revolve around coffee, or to be more exact -- around the café.

Every morning Portuguese in all corners of the country crawl out of bed and drink a coffee. But they don't drink it at home, nor do they drink it while driving to work. They stop at a café and do it properly. You see, this ritual of sorts must never be hurried or skipped.

Although I haven't been able to get into its spirit to the extent the Portuguese have – they have been practicing it for years and years – I have done it enough to see its merits.

In Cascais, a certain café became the perfect spot for executing my morning ceremony. *Sacolinha* (small bag) was its name. It originated with the establishment's beige paper bags used to wrap the freshly baked breads and pastries.

It was a medium sized café. Its black marble-like floor and tasteful lighting gave it a modern look.   A large L-shaped display counter, carrying hundreds of cakes, cookies and pastries of all sorts and kinds, was located in along the far walls. Eight small tables with glass tops occupied the rest of the space, leaving the customers and the waiter very narrow passageways.

The façade was made of large glass panes and offered an undisturbed view to the street while letting the natural light in. Outside, a covered terrace of sorts provided additional sitting room.

The row and clamor were astonishing for the number of people that were inside. With everyone talking animatedly, the banging of the dishes and the steam noises of the coffee machines, it sounded as if I was in an army cafeteria serving hundreds of soldiers. The one waiter who served the tables inside and outside, was rushing about with his tray.

I had to wait a few minutes before I could find a seat. Although there were four chairs around each table, I noticed that often only one person would occupy a table. Others would respect his privacy and would not sit down. A table freed up and I claimed it without delay.

People were passing through the doorway at an incredible rate. Almost every minute a new person would come in and another would leave. Most people went to the counter and had their coffee right there. At times there would be two rows of people standing along the glass display. Apparently, over a thousand customers visit *Sacolinha* every day.

Although I usually don't drink coffee, I have seen so many people drink it that I felt guilty writing a book about Portugal without at least trying the Portuguese coffee. I ordered one and the waiter looked at me blankly for some time.

"What's the matter?" I asked.

"Well, what kind would you like?" he asked politely but looked at me as if I had just landed from Mars.

"Just coffee," I replied with slight irritation.

"But, there are many kinds of coffees!" he argued. "Surely, you must specify which coffee you would like."

"All right, what do you have?" I asked. How many types of coffee could there be?

The waiter took a deep breath and arranged his thoughts before speaking. "First, we have the *café,* or *bica* as they call it in central and southern Portugal. It is an espresso coffee served in a demitasse. Then, there is the *bica pingada* which is the same but with a few drops of milk.

"A *carioca* is the same as a *café* but less concentrated. It has more water and thus is weaker than the *café*. An *italiana* is also a *café* but very strong, it has more coffee than water sometimes. The *garoto* is like a *bica pingada* but has a lot more milk," he took a deep breath and continued.

"One asks for a *meia de leite* when one wishes a coffee in a tea-cup sized cup. It means 'half full of milk,' and therefore consists of half-cup milk and the rest coffee. But, if you would like yet a larger coffee with some milk, you can order a *galão*. This one is served in a large and transparent glass the size of a water-glass, which might actually be quite hot when one picks it up."

I thought the torrent had passed and was about to thank him when he suddenly remembered another one. "Oh, and if you want your *galão* or *meia de leite* on the darker side, it is then *galão escuro* or *meia de leite escura*."

I meditated over the list. So many types of coffee! Which one should I have? I asked myself. The waiter stood there patiently, waiting to hear my choice.

"Er... I will take the first one on the list," I finally answered, unsure which one it was really.

"A *bica*? *Sim, senhora*," and he scurried away.

Men and women alike would come in, stand by the counter for five or ten minutes drinking their coffees and would then leave. Some were dressed elegantly; some came in casual shorts and T-shirt. I observed a few ladies to even arrive in gym clothes. The constant flow was amazing.

All of the tables were occupied and almost everyone was having lively conversations with everybody else. A couple was sitting outside reading the daily papers: a soccer newspaper for him and a People-like magazine for her. I looked at my watch and realized it was actually ten o'clock in the morning. Didn't they have to go to work? I wondered.

My *bica* arrived in a small white coffee cup on a small saucer. A colorful bag of sugar and a coffee-spoon were also included. The coffee was darker than the night and very hot. I carefully took a sip.

It was extremely concentrated, as if they took ten cups of American coffee and condensed it into the little white cup in front of me. The caffeine wave swept through my blood system. If one doesn't feel alert after one of those *bicas*, a visit to the doctor is highly recommended, I thought.

The waiter, Amadeu was his name, knew many of the customers by face. Each face seemed to have a special order connected with it and I watched as he would get them their regular order a moment after they sat down. He was very professional, efficient and smiled a lot.

I resolved that such a friendly and lively place was the perfect place to have a morning coffee and finished my *bica*. I thanked the waiter for his assistance and left him a nice tip. He smiled cheerfully and hurried on.

The morning ritual is not the end, but only the beginning. After all, there is still an entire day ahead offering many opportunities to visit the café.

The next *bica* is usually drunk after lunch and if one drank a lot of wine with the meal, two *bicas* might be a good idea. Then another *bica* is consumed during mid-afternoon and inevitably again after dinner.

The *café*, this excellent social drink often drunk either at a café or a restaurant, provides many opportunities to meet and chat with your friends. This is probably why

Portugal has the highest number of coffee shops and restaurants per capita in Europe!

The café is not only a place to go in the mornings. One time in spring, I spent a surfing week in a little coast town in the Alentejo with a few friends. We of course woke up around lunch and after a quick breakfast, loaded up the cars with the food, towels and surfboards.

We drove north for about ten minutes and then turned onto a dirt road that had more rocks, stones and holes than dirt. The narrow path led us along fields of wild plantation infrequently disturbed by small houses, to a dirt clearing at the edge of a cliff. The three or four other cars that were there, judged by the stickers on the back windows, obviously belonged to surfers.

We unpacked and, carrying our backpacks and surfboards, started the descent down to the beach. Though not too steep, it was enough to deter the masses and therefore when we reached the bottom, we found ourselves surrounded by a narrow strip of clean, white sand that stretched for kilometers with only a few groups of surfers and sunbathers here and there.

Ahead, the Atlantic Ocean waves formed long lines of foam along the coast while behind me, the cliffs rose sharply a hundred feet, their visible wavy and colorful rock formation layers forming breathtaking natural works of art.

"There are innumerable hidden beaches like that all over Portugal," explained my friend Gonçalo. "One just has to know where to look and be brave enough to drive there and climb down the cliffs – a task which usually seems a lot tougher than it actually is."

I looked around me in fascination. What an exotic place! It felt like we were on some island in the middle of the Pacific Ocean, far and away from any civilization (except perhaps the occasional dark wetsuit.) We surfed and sunbathed till the evening. We watched the stunning bright-orange giant fireball melt slowly and peacefully into the water, which marked the end of a great day at the beach.

I would strongly recommend to the reader, especially if you are in Portugal during the spring months, to set about finding your own beach along the western coast of Portugal. The unexplored beach is definitely something to experience.

After dinner which was around nine o'clock, we of course went to a small café in the village and met some friends who were also there unbeknownst to us. We lingered over several *cafés* and chatted for several hours. From there we went to another café, met other friends there and just sat around and talked for a while. By two o'clock we were ready to go to sleep.

I learned that if you want to go to see a movie, you first meet in a café, talk for a while and then as a group leave to the cinema. If there's a soccer game going on that afternoon, you meet your friends in the café and after a *bica*, go together to the game.

Some cafés, especially those situated on the beach or atop hills overlooking lovely scenic panoramas, also serve as a place where one can escape from the stress of life and relax for a while.

I remember one late afternoon, I was feeling a bit depressed and life didn't seem to be so grand. I hopped in my little car and drove off to a café located on the Marginal road near Estoril.

The balcony where white plastic tables and chairs were arranged neatly, was overlooking the sandy beach and the spacious ocean. Sitting there for nearly an hour, watching the relaxing view, mesmerized by the breaking waves, my attention drawn away occasionally by seagulls bickering over fish around the fishermen boats in the distance, the dark clouds over my head soon lifted and I found myself smiling.

In Portugal, I concluded, the café is the common meeting and relaxation place while the *café* is the social adhesive that brings people together.

From what I have seen, the Portuguese tend to go out often as opposed to staying at home. They adore sitting outside, breathing the fresh air, meeting their friends and above all, they love talking. And that, as opposed to sitting in front of the TV, is what I call life.

Now, one of life's secrets is which type of coffee to drink.

Avoiding the large enterprises that deal with mass quantities of ordinary coffee, I literally followed my nose to 'Casa Macário', a small specialty shop in the *Baixa* district in Lisbon. The strong smell of freshly ground coffee filled the old walking street and I was carried upon its wings to the doorstep.

The front of the store had a simple job of window

dressing done on it, a collection of wine and liquor bottles as well as various types of inviting chocolate boxes, which gave no clue of what was inside.

I stepped beyond the threshold into the small, dark room. Inside, a glass counter cased in wood provided a display of the best-imported chocolate bars and sweets. Shelves covered the entirety of each wall. To the right, they carried a vast array of different wines, from Port to Green Wine. Under the thick coat of dust upon most of them, I could discern the white lettering which gave away the vintage year for each wine. The youngest one was ten years old, and from there the years went back to the 1890's.

A hidden treasure, I whistled with admiration.

On the left, the shelves carried an assortment of different-sized and -colored boxes of world class mints, sourballs and licorice. Next, numerous thin bonbon packages stood aesthetically on their sides, their top covers announcing flavors, fillings and shapes. An extension of the counter had a larger display case offering a variety of candies by weight.

Though I couldn't easily find its source, the pervading aroma of coffee could be sensed in every corner of the store.

There were two employees behind the counter, both wearing the same light brown and red checkered shirt, which I concluded to be the work uniform in this small establishment.

One of them introduced himself as Fernando and offered his help. He had a fine mustache, a pleasant demeanor and spoke in a slow and calm manner.

"Well," I hesitated for a moment, trying to choose the right words for my question. "Is this shop, er...sponsored by any large company?"

The man unhurriedly blinked and smiled sagely, as if he knew exactly what my concern was. "No, it isn't. This shop was established in 1913 and has been in this location ever since. The owners are very happy with it and so are we. Not a lot changed over the last few decades."

I breathed with relief. To gain inside knowledge, the small, old-fashioned stores offered the best opportunities. Whereas in the big firms the workers have quotas, pressure and no time, the employees in the small shop are usually friendly, relaxed and have lots of time to answer my questions.

"What kinds of coffee do you have?" I asked.

Fernando turned around and pointed to a wide wooden cupboard. At the top were countless coffee makers and percolators, of varying sizes, shapes and colors. Beneath, a medley of brightly colored tin boxes of all sorts of tea was placed in neat rows across the shelves. The bottom part of the cupboard was a series of eight square boxes, each containing a different type of coffee beans. A tiny engraving above each box identified each kind.

"We have eight blends which we mix ourselves. The roasting is done by an outside company, but to our exact specifications. Here, we have the time and means to put the accent on quality," he said proudly. "You can buy our coffee and grind it at home or we can grind it for you here, as you wish."

In the background, senhor Zé, the other employee filled a small colorful sack with coffee beans from one of the boxes. He then rapidly folded its top over and over until the coffee inside was nicely packed, and with one swoosh of the hand tore a piece of sticky tape off the dispenser which sealed the paper sack. He handed the neatly packaged goods over to a customer with a smile.

"We were both in Angola during the war," explained Fernando, having noticed I was watching Zé's quick moves.   "There we became familiar with the coffee industry. After the war we soon found ourselves working in this shop. We have been at this for years," he said with a grin.

"Oh, the good old days," Zé joined the conversation. "I remember walking through the Angola fields in the baking sun," his unfocused stare stretched beyond my shoulder, "the warm drafts of wind caressing us and filling our lungs with wild fragrances of nature.

"We would often patrol along the coffee plantations where men hand-picked the grains, their wide straw hats protecting their heads from the unrelenting heat. And then back at the camp, one of the two existing airstrips served as a roasting factory; the coffee beans were scattered on top of the wide asphalt lane and left for hours to bake in the sun. Every so often the men would pass methodically along and turn the beans over.

"Sometimes," he added with a chuckle, "we would get bitten by coffee bugs. These small insects are common there. Once they bite, one usually gets a high fever that lasts for fifteen minutes or so and then disappears. If you saw someone stepping under a tree and resting for a quarter of an hour you knew that it was the coffee bugs at work."

"I love coffee," stated Fernando. "I drink a strong *bica* when I first wake up, another one around noon and one more after lunch. If I drink any more I can't sleep at night," he paused considering his statement. "But coffee is sometimes better than a beer or a glass of wine, in my opinion." He spoke earnestly and I was quite convinced. Working in such a store, how could one not like coffee?

A French couple walked in and asked for a specific liquor. Zé climbed a narrow ladder and got a bottle off one of the higher shelves. He came down with it and placed it in front of me. Suddenly, the bottle slowly started falling back and my hand instinctively shot out to grab it. But I was too late.

Both the French couple and I gasped as the bottle made a full loop and headed for the floor. But Fernando's quick hand grabbed it half way. He and Zé smiled at each other and we realized it was a rehearsed show. Fernando put the bottle in a plastic bag and handed it to the French couple. The man, still smiling at the trick, kissed the bottle that arrived in his hand in one piece. We all laughed.

I realized I was getting to like this store. The untroubled, peaceful atmosphere and the casual, unirritated fellows working there made me feel at home, and I was reluctant to leave.

"Do you mix the coffee here?" I tried to prolong the

conversation.

"Yes, we do. There is a basement below where we store, mix and grind the coffee. Would you like to see it?" Zé offered. I accepted the offer without hesitation.

Zé asked Miguel, another older employee who was working in the back room, to show me around the basement. Miguel smiled and slowly motioned me to follow him. We descended a set of creaky wooden stairs to the lower level.

The basement was a sizeable room, lit by the hard illumination of a single light bulb that hung from the ceiling. Large canvass sacks of different shades of brown were stacked high on top of wooden platforms, all the way to the ceiling and along the walls.

Isolated bags stood erect on the floor, their tops open, revealing the beans inside.

"These are the different types of coffee beans we use. Here are the Brazilian coffees," he pointed at the darker sacks at the corner and went on to describe the rest. These were Colombian, Mexican, Angolan coffees as well as other specialty ones from exotic islands.

"Coffee is usually composed of two types of beans, *robusta* and *arabica*. *Robusta* is the more common bean that is not so rich in flavor. The *arabica* is the more expensive bean that gives the coffee its strength and savor. The *robusta* gives more body to the coffee and more importantly, brings out the taste of the *arabica*. Most coffees blend a lot of *robusta* with a little *arabica*.

"In that respect, most of our blends differ greatly from the norm. Take the São Tome blend, for example," he picks up a handful of the dark, perfectly roasted beans and hands it to me. "This is a very special coffee, which is made of five portions of *arabica* and one portion of *robusta* from Angola. It's very strong.

"And this one," he picked another handful from a different sack and placed it in my other hand, "is the best we have. The *Augusta* blend. It is made of four portions of Kenyan coffee, one portion of Colombian and one portion of São Tome."

I smelled the beans and was surprised they had no aroma.

"Only when you grind it does the savor come out," Miguel explained. He stepped across the room with me trailing behind, and entered a smaller room divided off by a partition made of wood and glass. "Here is where we grind it."

The pleasant aroma hung around like a cloud inside this miniature improvised room. Several large machines stood there immobile and quiet. "They are used mainly in the mornings to grind the coffee freshly each day," Zé commented. "And that about covers everything!" he said with a smile.

I thanked him very much for the tour and we climbed back upstairs.

Fernando greeted me again, unhurriedly.

"Here, try our São Tome blend," he said and reached for a nearby white coffee machine. He pressed a button and it started to rattle and spew. A moment later, he handed me a small cup with the dark, nearly-boiling liquid inside.

The hot vapors spreading into the air had an intense, sweet odor which I couldn't resist from breathing in a few times. I sipped cautiously and the pungent taste of strong coffee permeated my mouth. Unlike the usual *bicas* one gets in a café, this one had a smoother and richer taste which rolled in one's mouth and left a long, pleasant aftertaste.

"Now try the *Augusta* blend," he said and pressed another button. After a moment of noisy activity, the small machine which automatically grinds and prepares the coffee inside, produced another *bica*. The aroma of the *Augusta* was so strong that I could smell it as the coffee was being poured into the cup.

Its taste was exquisite. It wasn't stronger than the São Tome, but its flavor was delicious and unmistakably unique. After such a *bica*, it is hard to go back to regular coffee, I reflected. I bought a bag of it to take home.

I thanked them all and promised I would be back soon. They smiled and went back to practicing their tricks.

On the way back, the strong aroma of the ground *Augusta* soon filtered its way slowly out of its wrapping. None of the bags and sacks that wrapped it could hold back the fragrance. I eventually gave in, opened the bag and let the aroma fill the car. Breathing in the fresh coffee aroma and energized by the two *bicas* in my bloodstream, I began to really understand the song I had mentioned earlier. Life was indeed wonderful after all.

EPILOGUE

With every sunrise and sunset in Portugal, I have stumbled across new subjects which are worth writing about. There are so many interesting people, so many enchanting places and so many intriguing traditions there.

But I feel that every person has his own individual viewpoint and way of experiencing things. In that respect, Europe's best-kept secret holds a treasure which no one but you can unravel. And this treasure is your own story of personal discovery in this fascinating country.

It was my intention to share the inside knowledge I had gathered during my lengthy visits in Portugal with the hope of sparking an interest in the Portuguese, their unique old-fashioned lifestyle and heart-warming traditions. Portugal, in a way, has been asleep for several centuries until it woke up only two decades ago and following its recent acceptance into the European Community began developing rapidly.

My only fear is that with development will come loss

of tradition, and although it is rather optimistic and even naïve on my part, I must express my wish that Portugal finds a way to achieve the former without the latter.

For example, I have heard of regulations in the city of Porto which forbade a certain fast food franchise to paste its screaming red and yellow colors all over their newly purchased property in the centuries-old Avenida dos Aliados. And I applaud for that. Though I have nothing against fast food franchises, I can't help but bear a grudge against anyone destroying ancient cultural sites. That fast food restaurant did eventually open, but its owners preserved the old décor inside and in that way contributed a little to preserving the Portuguese heritage.

Another example exists in the Alentejo, that extraordinary stretch of wild and varied vegetation which is the natural habitat of the *alentejano*. In many of its rural areas, laws prohibit building new houses and only allow renovation or reconstruction.

For some this might appear as an utter waste: think about all the new houses that could be erected, think about the possible increase in the employment, they say with green neon dollar signs flashing across their minds. But for me these laws are a blessing from above. I think solely about the beauty of nature in the Alentejo, the relaxed life there and about the rare human species which inhabit its rolling hills. This region could well be one of the only ones still in existence in our world today and deserves to be protected. If one doesn't like it, then one shouldn't buy land there.

The majority of the people in Portugal depend on

manual agriculture for their survival. In Portugal's many small *mini-mercados* one can usually find only fresh fruit and vegetables that have been picked straight from a small farmer's back yard. As I see it, these people should be assisted with government incentives; manual cultivation of the land is a rare asset which Portugal should encourage.

In addition, I find it fascinating to tour a country where I can enjoy the good things in life without having to constantly worry about my inability to speak the Portuguese language being taken advantage of, getting my car stripped at night or getting robbed at gunpoint. And honestly, I was surprised at how many nice adventures and very few mishaps I experienced.

Though I am not saying that Portugal is a hundred percent crime-free, and one should take sensible precautions like not visibly leaving anything in one's car and locking one's doors at night while there, crime in Portugal is not a prevalent threat.

There is something magical and mystical about Portugal, besides the spellbinding landscape. If one is willing to stretch one's patience a few inches and not expect things to happen instantly, one will find that the majority of the people are friendly, sincere and relaxed -- unusual qualities that one can't find any more in many corners of the globe.

During my visits, I have attempted to mingle with Portuguese, to participate in their traditions and to understand them better. Really, the language barrier is not what it is made out to be. I encourage you to talk, participate and understand for yourself. And maybe you will find yourself just like I did, taking home with you a new, more relaxing viewpoint on life.

This little near-heaven country could possibly become a center of exploration voyages once again just like it was in the fifteenth century. Only this time the discovery journeys will not be to Africa or to India but into ourselves; the prizes will not be of gold and spices but of the peaceful and easy-going qualities that we so often forget we possessed.

I earnestly wish you the best of luck in enjoying Europe's best-kept secret: Portugal!

Pronunciation Guide

Notes: ^ symbolizes accent. "j" is the 'dg' sound in "orange" but with the 'd' sound.

Alentejano [alent^janu] – an inhabitant of the Alentejo region.
Alface [al^fa-sé] – lettuce.
Auto-estrada [auto sht^radé] – highway.

Baba de camelo [^baba de camé-^lu] – a Portuguese mousse-like dessert.
Baixa [^bai-sha] – the downtown area in Lisbon.
Bandarilha [ban-da-^ril-ya] – the spear-like objects used by the bullgfighters.
Barriga de freira [bar-^riga de frei-^ra] – a Portuguese dessert made with eggs.
Beijinhos [bei-^jinsh] – greeting kisses.
Belém [be-^lei] – a section of Lisbon, the Portuguese word for Bethlehem.
Boas festas [bo-^ahsh   ^fesh-tash] – happy holidays.
Boa tarde [bo-^ah   ^tard] – good afternoon.
Boca do Inferno [^bo-ca do in-^fer-nu] – a place near

Cascais, "the mouth of hell."
Bombeiros [bom-^bei-rush] – a firefighter.
Bom dia [bo(n) ^dee-ia] – good morning.
Boné [bo-^né] – a type of old-fashioned cap.

Café [ca-^fé] – coffee, usually refers to a type served in a small cup.
Cabo do Roca [^ca-bu do ro-^ca] – a place near Sintra, the most western point in Europe.
Caldo verde [cal-^du   ^ver-de] – a type of vegetable soup with a few pieces of meat.
Capa [ca-^pa] – the assistant to the bullfighters who carry the colorful capes.
Capuchos [ca-^pu-chus] – hoods.
Carioca de Limão [ca-rio-^ca de li-^mau] – a type of hot drink with lemon.
Cascais [ca-sh-^ca-eesh] – a town near Lisbon.
Caveleiro [^ca-ve-leiru] – the horse-mounted bullfighter.
Colega [co-^le-ga] – colleague.
Convento [^con-ven-tu] – convent/monastery.

De nada [de ^na-da] – "You're welcome."
Doces [^do-ses] – sweets.
Dom [dom] – a title of nobility.
Dona [^do-na] – "Mrs."

E′ pá [e-^pa] – a word of exclamation.
Escuro [esh-^cu-ru] – dark.
Escudo [esh-^cu-du] – the monetary unit of Portugal.
Estrada [esh-^tra-da] – street.

Fado [fa-^du] – traditional (usually sad) songs.
Fartura [far-^tu-ra] – a type of a fried dough snack.
Fios de ovos [^fee-ius de ^o-vush] – a dessert made of sweet egg strands.
Forcado [for-^ca-du] – the bullfighter who has to catch the bull with his bare hands.

Galão [ga-^la-au] – coffee with milk served in a large glass.
Garoto [^ga-ro-tu] – coffee with a lot of milk served in a semitasse.
Guincho [^guin-shoo] – a famous beach near Cascais.

Lulas da sevilhana [^loo-lash da ^se-vil-iana] – deep fried squid.

Marginal [^mar-ji-nal] – a road between Lisbon and Cascais.
Meia de leite [^me-ya de ^lei-te] – coffee served in a teacup with a lot of milk.
Mercado [^mer-ca-du] – market.
Miradouro [mi-ra-^dough-ru] – a place of scenic view, usually with shaded benches.
Moscatel de Setúbal [^moosh-ca-tel de Se-^tu-bal] – a special Portuguese wine from Setúbal.
Muito [mui-^tu] – a lot, much.

Não [^now] – no, negative.

Obrigada [o-bri-^ga-da] – thank you (said by a woman.)
Obrigado [o-bri-^ga-du] – thank you (said by a man.)
Ovos [^o-vush] – eggs.

Pão de Deus [^pow de Dee-^ius] – a type of pastry.
Papos de anjo [^pa-pus   de ^an-ju] – an egg-type dessert.
Pasteis [^pash-teish] – a small cup-like pastry.
Pastelaria [pash-^tle-reeia] – a shop selling pastry and cakes.
Peixe [pei-^sh-e] – fish.
Ponte [^pon-te] – bridge.
Praia [^pra-ya] – beach.

Queijada [kei-^ja-da] – a sweet cheese pastry.
Queijaria [kei-^ja-ree-ya] – a place where cheese is made or sold.
Queijo [kei-^ju] – cheese.
Quinta [^kin-ta] – a large estate.

Santo António [^san-tu an-^ton-iu] – Saint Anthony.
São João [^sa-au ju-^wow] – Saint John.
São Pedro [^sa-au ^ped-ru] – Saint Peter.
Sempre em frente [^semp-re a ^fren-te] – straight ahead.
Senhor [sen-^ior] – "Mr."
Serra [^se-rra] – a mountain range.

Tasca [^tash-ca] – an inexpensive traditional restaurant.
Tio Manel [tiu ^ma-nel] – uncle Manel.
Touro [toi-^ru] – a bull.

Tortas [^tor-tash] – slices of foamy cake.
Toucinho do céu [too-^shi-nu do she-^eu] – a dessert made of eggs and marzipan.
Travesseiro [tra-ve-^ssei-ru] – a type of sweet pastry. Means "pillow."
Trouxas de ovos [tro-^shash de ^o-vush] – an egg dessert.

Vinho do casa [^vin-iu do ^ca-sa] – the wine of the house.
Vinho verde [^vin-iu ^ver-de] – green wine.

BIBLIOGRAPHY

* A NEW HISTORY OF PORTUGAL
H.V. Livermore – Cambridge University Press
1966

HISTÓRIA DE PORTUGAL
José Hermano Saraiva – Alfa Publishing,1983

THE LOVELIEST TOWNS AND VILLAGES IN
PORTUGAL
Júlio Gil – Editorial Verbo, 1991

PORTUGAL – A WINE COUNTRY
Francisco Esteves Gonçalves – Editora Potuguesa De
Livros Técnicos e Científicos,
1984

* THE PERFECT PRINCE
Elaine Sanceau – Livraria Civiliaçao Editora,
1959

THE PORTUGUESE – THE LAND AND ITS PEOPLE
Marion Kaplan – Penguin Books, 1991

For other books by Sar Perlman search Amazon.

The End

Made in the USA
Coppell, TX
16 June 2021

57441588R30152